ROAR FROM ZION

"My dear friend and covenant brother of forty years has written a new book. *Roar from Zion* reveals Paul Wilbur's heart and passions. There is the desire for intimacy in worship, for revival, for sharing the truth about Yeshua with our Jewish people, and for the recovery of the Jewish historic and prophetic context of the Scriptures. In addition, this new book describes the new mandate Celebration Church in Jacksonville, Florida, has been pursuing for a living experience with Yeshua, the Son of David and the Son of God."

—Asher Intrater, president of Tikkun Global and
Revive Israel

"This book tells the amazing story about an amazing event that took place in Jerusalem and about the amazing roar from Zion. At times, it felt like I was reading a novel, but the story is real, and the message is real. God will yet again roar from Zion, and the Jewish people, along with the whole world, will be shaken. Read this book and join this end-time spiritual journey for yourself!"

—Dr. Michael L. Brown, host of *The Line of Fire* radio
broadcast

"If you enjoy Paul Wilbur's music, messages, and writings, as I do, you will enjoy this latest release, *Roar from Zion*,

"The reader will be enlightened by Paul's insight into the Sabbath—and why and how it is meant to be celebrated. He shares the importance of remembering God's feasts and festivals and

why God has given them to us, His family. Deep into the text, he also reminds us of the importance of daily Bible reading, prayer, fasting, fellowship, and family. Personal revelations on the power of praise and worship are shared by this musician and artist in a way that testifies to Paul's more than forty years of service.

"*Roar from Zion* is a heartfelt and challenging encouragement as we prepare for God to restore His Kingdom, when He will roar from Zion and thunder from Jerusalem."

—John Arthur Muenz Jr., M.D., Jacksonville, Florida

"The word 'vocation'—as in 'ministerial vocation'—comes from the Latin *vocatio*, meaning 'voice.' People notice impulses within them that incline them toward various vocations—could be a plumber, electrician, doctor, housewife, or teacher. The point is that people notice something in them that wants to be heard—thus a 'vocation.' While granting the value of all legitimate vocations, there's something particularly noteworthy about hearing the voice of God and then responding accordingly.

"*Roar from Zion* tells the story of how a man walked my talk: Paul Wilbur heard something, responded, and the rest is history—i.e., his story. Having its genesis in a 'still small voice,' *Roar from Zion* is its author's autobiographical journey through time and circumstance. It tells the story of God at work in the world today and the emergence of a distinctively Jewish-Christian worship experience—with Paul very much in the vanguard. He gives a window into his life and his ministry calling's vicissitudes, and, with it, a culminating vision for the basics of a 'one new man' congregational model planted in a contemporary church experience.

"This book is full of inspiration and information. It's creatively loaded with biblical stories and applications, and I am so very pleased to commend it to you."

—Dr. Jeffrey Seif, University Distinguished Professor of Bible and Jewish Studies at the King's University-Houston, a member of the TLV Bible Translation Team, a former chair of the Department of Jewish Studies at the Christ for the Nations Institute, and host of *Our Jewish Roots* on Daystar Television and TBN

ROAR FROM ZION

ROAR
FROM
ZIN

Discovering the Power of Jesus
through Ancient Jewish Traditions

PAUL WILBUR

SALEM
BOOKS
an imprint of Regnery Publishing
Washington, D.C.

Salem Books™ is a trademark of Salem Communications Holding Corporation

Regnery' is a registered trademark and its colophon is a trademark of Salem Communications Holding Corporation

Cataloging-in-Publication data on file with the Library of Congress

ISBN: 978-1-68451-090-0
eISBN: 978-1-68451-100-6

Library of Congress Control Number: 2020952243

Published in the United States by
Salem Books
An Imprint of Regnery Publishing
A Division of Salem Media Group
Washington, D.C.
www.SalemBooks.com

Manufactured in the United States of America

10 9 8 7 6 5 4 3 2 1

Books are available in quantity for promotional or premium use. For information on discounts and terms, please visit our website: www.SalemBooks.com.

CONTENTS

Foreword   xi

SECTION 1
DECLARATION OF THE WORD

Chapter 1: The Roar   3

Chapter 2: A Call in the Night   13

Chapter 3: A House Divided   29

SECTION 2
DEMONSTRATION OF THE SPIRIT

Chapter 4: The Day Jesus Came to Church   41

Chapter 5: As It Is in Heaven   51

SECTION 3
ACTIVATION OF THE COVENANT AND HIS KINGDOM

Chapter 6: The Sabbath   65

Chapter 7: The Healing of the Table   79

Chapter 8: A Double-Edged Sword   87

Chapter 9: A New Era Dawning   107

Chapter 10: Taste and See   123

Chapter 11: United We Stand   141

Afterword   155

Appendix: Feasts of the Kingdom   157

FOREWORD

Worship is the reality of the relationship between God, the Creator and Possessor of Heaven and Earth, and mankind. Yeshua defined the experience of worship in John 4:23–24: "But the time is coming and is already here when the true worshipers will worship the Father in spirit [from the heart, the inner self] and in truth; for the Father seeks such people to be His worshipers. God is spirit [the Source of life, yet invisible to mankind], and those who worship Him must worship in spirit and truth" (AMP). Truly, this defines the reality of the relationship between God and man.

This book by Paul Wilbur is real! *Roar from Zion* is an amazing journey from self to reality. This is one of the few books that you hear instead of read. You sense reality from the first sentence through the closing paragraph. In *Roar from Zion*, Paul led me on a journey into the reality of worship in his life and the reality of a Holy God. I found myself worshiping. I entered into knowing the Lord and experiencing His heart and His character with a depth of understanding that was new and fresh.

"The Lord will thunder and roar from Zion!" (Joel 3:16 AMP). As we are proceeding in this new era in history, we must look and listen for the "new." This new era will be summarized as "the era in history when the Lord roared from Heaven!" He is listening for those in the Kingdom of God who will echo this same roar from Earth. This book will help you develop and unlock the sound that has been stored within you for NOW!

In the days ahead, there will be divine alignments and moments of change that will produce faith explosions in the Lord's people. The Lord says, "I have power within you that I will explode!" You have a sound that will reflect that power. *Roar from Zion* will help you learn to better understand that sound. This will be the sound of "One New Man" in the earth.

In a recent gathering, I shared, "We will be in a great tension—a new era of warfare for us. It won't be like the warfare we've been in, in the past. It's a tension arising which I call 'The Lion vs. the Dragon War.' That will happen this decade. We must know who we are part of. We must leave our maintenance mentality and walk into a conquest mentality based upon the boundaries God is assigning to each one of us. This is a word I want to leave with each one of us—individually, corporately, territorially, and generationally."

We go from faith to faith, glory to glory, and strength to strength. A new strength is coming into our inner being. This strength will result in the "Sound of FAITH" being expressed. New vision is arising. Strength means "the battle to withstand attack." While reading *Roar from Zion*, I sensed new strength arising in my bones.

Deliverers will rise up! Entire groups of people will begin to be delivered from the bondage and oppression that has kept them prostrate, and they will begin to stand before the Lord with great shouts of victory. This is a time of much confrontation. But we can be assured of victory when our confrontation with the enemy comes from a place of intimate communion and worship. This is a time when we must give Judah (our praise and worship) the freedom to experiment until we come into the sound that will bring victory into the earthly realm. We must distinguish the sound of Judah. "The LORD also will roar from Zion…the heavens and earth will shake…the LORD will be a shelter for His people, and the strength of the children of Israel" (Joel 3:16 NKJV).

God roars as He goes to battle. He will roar against His covenant enemies. His covenant people will also begin to roar and become a fearful, holy remnant to contend with in the earthly realm. He will be a shelter and a strength to those who respond to His sound and call on Him. Worship this season will determine how the multitudes in the valley of decision begin to decide to follow God. There is an inherited roar within you. Let the Lord draw you near and develop that roar within you so that this sound is brought forth at the appropriate time in your life.

Sound creates movement. Heaven and Earth are going through many great transitions. As God's people, we are the central theme of the transition. Transition means crossing over from one place or dimension to another. Transition is also a shift in sound, a musical modulation, or a passage leading from one section of a piece to another.

Your conscience is like a window between soul and spirit. Make sure nothing is clouding your conscience in this season. Sound that leads you into movement and worship will cause your conscience to remain in alignment with God. Your conscience is one of the absolute authorities of your life. When your conscience is aligned and interacting with the Word of God, the "window" remains clean and open. The conscience is the lamp of the body. The conscience is the eye of our spirit that causes us to see into the heavenly realms.

We say what we see! Open your mouth and release the decree that is in your heart! This is the season of confession and decree. What we say now determines our future. If we will cleanse our consciences, then the revelation that has not been able to influence our minds will find entrance.

Let the shout of the Lord arise in you. Let your confidence in the Lord be heard. Though the enemy is roaming like a mighty lion, seeking whom he may destroy, there is a roar in you to be released at this time. This roar will defy the enemy. Go past that which seems invincible in your life. Get in the river of change that is flowing by your door and let it take you to your next place. Get a shield of protection around you and birth the new that the Lord has for you. Your latter end (future) will be greater than your beginning!

There is a violent sound arising in the earth. This is the sound of God's people praising! As you praise "violently," you are releasing the "Roar of the Lord" that has been held captive in God's people. God's sound emanates from Heaven and orders much of what goes on in the earthly realm. When He is ready to bring restoration to Earth, He releases His sound. Judah goes first! Judah roars! The roar of God is within us.

Judah means "Praise Yahweh." Do not resist the major shift that is recreating the way we worship and our corporate acknowledgment of God. "Yahweh" means "the God of covenant." Our praise and worship are important to the Lord. Revelation 5:5 tells us that Jesus is the Lion of Judah. That Lion is living in us. Satan only roams about "like" a roaring lion. Jesus *is* a roaring lion. We have to let that aspect of praise be in us. That Lion in us is strong, confident, and aggressive. "'They will walk after the LORD, He will roar like a lion; indeed He will roar" (Hosea 11:10 NASB). There is a sound of God's being released in the earth right now through His people that is signifying the strength of God in these times. The enemy is walking around like a roaring lion seeking whom he will devour, sounding accusations and producing fear. But at the same time, God is releasing His roar, which is much greater than the enemy's.

The Lord is saying: "Let Me bring forth a new expression of worship. Let it take you beyond where you have been with Me before. I have increased My activity in the heavens, and there is a new release of the angelic forces that are My Triumphant Reserve for just this— your time in history! Don't allow the stirring of the second heaven to cause you to shrink back. Instead, rush toward the Roar of Heaven that I Am releasing in this hour. This is an Awakening Roar, a Declaration of War Roar, and a Releasing Roar that will cause keys of revelation to unlock the treasures of the ages—treasures held for you and treasures planted in you. Remember the last chapters of My Covenant Book—YOU WIN! For I AM the One who has NEVER LOST A BATTLE!"

Roar from Zion will help you see God's Kingdom come in its fullness. We must understand how to pray and position ourselves for the future. Get ready for a great shaking! Thrones of iniquity are going to fall. We are about to see a tremendous shift in worship throughout the world as God's throne is reestablished and the Church rises into a new glory. One New Man is arising! A King is coming! Join Paul Wilbur as he helps us understand how to pray, watch, and express the sound of our future.

Dr. Chuck D. Pierce
President of Glory of Zion International Ministries
President of Global Spheres, Inc.

SECTION 1

DECLARATION OF THE WORD

CHAPTER 1

THE ROAR

Write the vision and make it plain....
—*Habakkuk 2:2 (NKJV)*

Have you ever found yourself turning the last page of a very long chapter in your life and asking, "Now what?" That is exactly where I landed when my twenty-seven-year-long relationship with Integrity Music came to an end.

It was a bittersweet time for me, as our partnership had produced some of my life's best musical works for God's Kingdom. Live recordings in Israel like *Shalom Jerusalem, Jerusalem Arise, Lion of Judah,* and *Desert Rain* were all created with my friends at Integrity Music. Other projects like "Up to Zion," "Holy Fire," and "The Watchman" were considered groundbreaking releases, mainstream worship materials that helped create a new genre. The company had invested millions of dollars to create the records and videos that the world would use to worship the King of Israel in many languages and nations. But that chapter in my life was drawing to a close. So, with a touch of sadness, I found myself asking that age-old question: Now what?

It was then that I got a call from a relatively new friend who asked what I was going to do now and stated that he had been praying for me and the ministry. He wanted to be a blessing if he could. His passion for me and my family was a wonderful surprise. I was utterly amazed when he offered to fly from Ohio to my home in Jacksonville, Florida, and invest a couple of days in praying and planning with us.

We covered a lot of ground in those two days, asking a lot of necessary questions which begged for really good answers. Questions like: *How long do you plan to keep up the 225 travel days every year? What happens to your family ministry if one of those flights takes a detour to Heaven? What about the future of your two sons, who have dedicated themselves to you and the ministry?*

Finally, after two intensive days of prayer and discussion, the word came. "Build me a Blackbird," the Lord said.

That meant something to me—but for everyone else, let me explain. Back in the 1960s, the first U.S. spy plane, called the U-2, was shot down over the Soviet Union. The Cold War with Russia was in full bloom at the time, and this incident was a major disaster for the United States and the entire free world. Fortunately, the pilot survived. After some intense negotiations, the U.S. wound up exchanging a Soviet spy for one of our own. This gripping story was brought to life on the screen by Tom Hanks in the film *Bridge of Spies*.

The end result for America was that a team of the very best minds in aeronautics, physics, mathematics, and engineering was assembled in a secret location and commissioned to design a plane that would fly higher and faster than anything the world had ever seen. The goal was to build a spy plane that would be invulnerable to all kinds of weapons from the ground or air and put the U.S. back in the lead of technology and top-secret information gathering. The result was the

Blackbird SR-71. It exceeded even the highest expectations. When it was retired many years later, it remained unrivaled in stealth, speed, and technical abilities.

After hearing from God, we knew what we were supposed to do: build a Blackbird. But what would our Blackbird look like? What would it sound like? Would it make any sound at all?

Then suddenly, one day, it came to me in stark black and white— the blueprints for our new mission.

The morning started out like any other normal day at home as I tried to catch up after being gone for several days. The day was packed, but I wanted to have a few minutes with my Bible to hear the voice of the Lord. I knew I only had a few minutes, and I wanted to make them count. I chose to read something for context, not just a random Psalm or two. I had been missing our son Joel and his wife, Sharon, since they had moved to Los Angeles several years before. Thoughts of him took me to the book of Joel with its three short chapters.

I breezed through Chapter 1, then on through Chapter 2. The locusts were devouring everything: "They swarm over the city and run along its walls. They enter all the houses, climbing like thieves through the windows" (Joel 2:9 NLT). Next came the promise of the outpouring of the Spirit of God that Peter declared fulfilled in Acts 2 during the Feast of Shavuot (Pentecost). Then came the judgment of the nations for dividing up "My land" and scattering "My people." As I read those words, I wondered how so many people (even well-meaning Christians) could support the "Two-State Solution," which claims that a Palestinian state should be created alongside Israel to accommodate Arabs, who occupied the land in 1948. The "solution" involves taking land from Israel to create the Palestinian state, thus further dividing the nation.

Then I saw it, right there in Joel 3:14–16 (NIV):

> Multitudes, multitudes in the valley of decision. For the
> Day of the Lord is near.... The Lord will ROAR from Zion,
> and thunder from Jerusalem.

I had read those verses many times before, but they had never hit
me quite so hard as at that moment. First, I thought of the "multitudes" of lives hanging in the balance between Heaven and Hell. The
day is quickly approaching when all people on Earth will be judged
for their sins and the mistreatment of Israel, the firstborn child of
God's covenant family. Then, somehow it seemed a sound would
come from the Judge of the Nations and Protector of His People—a
ROAR from the Lion of Judah. His thundering voice would push back
the darkness, repelling fear and the invaders of the Holy City. Finally,
there would be peace—*shalom*—for the people of God and His holy
hill, Mount Zion.

I sat for just a few moments more, stunned at what I had just
seen and heard. Then that inner voice spoke: "Put together a team
of anointed worshipers and players, release the sound in Jerusalem
during the Feast of Tabernacles in 2018 (the seventieth anniversary
of the State of Israel, the fiftieth anniversary of Jerusalem as Israel's
undivided capital, the hundredth anniversary of the Balfour Declaration, and the five hundredth anniversary of the Protestant Ref-
ormation). Lift up a sound and I will roar from Zion and thunder
from Jerusalem."

The Blackbird now had a shape and a voice. The secret location
to build it? Jerusalem.

THUNDER FROM JERUSALEM

I wondered what the roar and thunder would sound like and what the impact would be on the earth. In Joel 3, the sound of this Voice causes the earth to shake and the mountains to tremble, but that same Voice is "a refuge for His people, a stronghold for the people of Israel" (Joel 3:16 NIV). I find it interesting that even though the English word *people* appears twice in this verse, the Hebrew words used in the original text are different.

The first word used for "people" is *am*, and it appears more than 1,900 times in the Bible. It refers to a large group of people who share a common purpose and goal. The second Hebrew word used for "people" here is *ben* (son), and that appears almost 5,000 times in the Bible. It refers to people by reason of relationship, whether natural or adopted. It specifically speaks of the children of Israel.

Because this particular passage is speaking about the Day of the Lord, the day that the Messiah returns to defend Jerusalem and judge the earth, I believe this verse speaks about His covering protection for both Israel *and* the Ecclesia (the Church). All members of His family that call on His Name in holiness are included in this promise.

That roar is the voice of the Holy One of Israel. As I searched through the pages of my Bible, I found it again and again. I discovered the roar in Amos 1 and 3. Turn back just a few pages and there it is again in Hosea 11. *Wow,* I thought, *Why haven't I seen this before?*

This sound is a shield and a fortress for the people of God, but it is also a declaration of devastation against the darkness. The roar of Zion plunges the enemy into profound confusion and destroys the invading forces. The sound that gives life to His people also brings utter devastation and death to His enemies. Now I wondered,

Was this the same sound that delivered Jehoshaphat and all of Judah from the three invading armies in 2 Chronicles 20? And what about the "thunder" heard in 1 Samuel 7 that chased the Philistines away? Might this also have been the sound that crumbled the mighty walls of Jericho?

In the case of the Philistines' defeat described in 1 Samuel, the Ark of the Covenant had been returned to Israel and rested there for some twenty years. Under Samuel's leadership, the Israelites had put away all their idols and served the Lord only, but they were still under the boot of the Philistines. When Israel cried out to Samuel for deliverance, he told the people to assemble at Mizpah. There he drew water and poured it out before the Lord. In a desert environment, water means life or death, and so this offering of water symbolized their total reliance on God.

They also fasted, put away all their idols, and confessed their sins. When the Philistines heard Israel had returned to the worship of YHVH, they were alarmed and assembled their army to put an end to this revival. Samuel responded to the invasion by building an altar, sacrificing a lamb, and crying out to the Lord on Israel's behalf. The word for "crying out" is the Hebrew word *za'ak*, which means "to cry out by reason of affliction, distress, and issuing a summons for help." And what was Heaven's response?

> But that day the Lord thundered (*ra-am*) with a great thunder (*ra'am gadol*) against the Philistines and threw them into such a panic that they were routed before the Israelites. The men of Israel rushed out of Mizpah and pursued the Philistines, slaughtering them along the way.... So the

Philistines were subdued and did not invade Israelite territory again. (1 Samuel 7:10–13 NASB)

The first Hebrew word, *ra-am*, means "to thunder, to roar, God's voice of judgment especially in meting out military confusion against His enemies." The latter expression, *ra'am gadol*, is a combination of both *ra-am* and *gadol*, which means "big or great"—the combined meaning being "a great thunder or roar."

ANOTHER SOUND

The response from Heaven described in 2 Chronicles 20, when God delivered His people from three invading armies, is similar, yet the sound from the people of God is quite different. Rather than a shout or cry of distress or anguish, they offered up a loud shout of praise (*t'hillah*, which is derived from *hallal*, the adoration and thanksgiving that men render to YHVH) and worship, saying, "Give thanks to the LORD, for he is good. His love endures forever" (Psalm 136:1 NIV). Although the Scriptures do not tell us about a responding sound of thunder or roaring in this passage, the results are exactly the same. The invading army heard a sound that caused all of them to be thrown into such confusion and panic that they took up their swords and slaughtered each other.

When I took out my Hebrew Bible, I discovered another amazing thing. The word used for "roar" in Joel 3:16 is the word *sha'ag*, and it has two meanings or sounds associated with it. One definition is "a cry or shout of despair." Yet in the same sentence, it is also defined as "a roar of victory or judgment." I confess that I was confused. *What in the world? I have never seen a word defined in the same sentence with two such seemingly opposing meanings.* As I sat there wondering how this all worked, I heard that inner voice again: *When you shout or cry out in despair, I roar over you in victory.*

The thought of sounds we make on the earth provoking the thunder and roar from Heaven's throne room captivated me. *So, if we get this right,* I thought, *many could be won to the Lord, darkness and death would be pushed back, the "multitudes in the valley of decision" would choose Life, Israel would be saved, and hope would be released to the nations.*

But how could we possibly make such a sound? The answer was obvious: we would release the covenant cry for help and praise, and God would release the Thunder and the Roar of victory.

WHAT'S IN A SOUND?

A big question concerning this revelation of sound is simply: *Why*? Consider that in both Matthew 7:11 and again in Luke 11:13, Jesus says, "If you then, though you are evil, know how to give good gifts to your children, how much more will your Father in Heaven give the Holy Spirit to those who *ask* (*aiteō*, request, beg, cry out to) Him?"

Every good parent knows the sounds their children make. As our two sons grew, we quickly identified the different sounds that came from their cribs. The happy gurgling sounds told us all was well; the "I'm hungry" or "please change my diaper" sounds got a response when needed. We even recognized the "I am angry" cry that sometimes went unanswered during the temper tantrums all babies try on new parents.

But the one cry that *never* went unheeded was the sound of despair, anguish, or pain. It solicited an immediate and impassioned response from both me and my wife—a loud cry of something like a roar or thunder that meant "Daddy's coming." The distance between us and that crib would vanish in milliseconds as we brought all our power and resources to help our child.

So "if you who are evil" (compared to our Heavenly Father) "know how to give good things to your children"—or know how to respond to your own children's cries for help—"how much more will your Heavenly Father give?" Our role was to cry out to Him and trust Him to respond as the loving Father that He is.

One final question remained as our mission began to take shape: *Why me?*

They say music is "the language of the soul" at the "heart of man," the "international language" we all share. Music has the power to calm the rage of a savage beast, to woo the heart of a lover, and so much more. There has never been a culture in which music has not played a significant role in day-to-day life or expression.

I have heard it said that every move of the Spirit of God needs someone to preach it and—you guessed it—someone to sing it. It seems God had chosen us to do just that. In fact, as I look back over my life story, I can see His hand preparing us to walk with Him "for such a time as this."

CHAPTER 2

A Call in the Night

M y story began on a frigid winter day in January 1951 at Lowell General Hospital just outside Boston, Massachusetts. My mother was a registered nurse there, so we were given the best space available for my grand entrance. My Jewish dad was a chemist for a major chemical and dye company. He quickly rose to become a junior manager with an office in downtown Manhattan, so the company moved us to northern New Jersey in 1960.

As Dad climbed the corporate ladder, our family of five—two boys five years apart with a sister wedged in between—moved quite often. Every time, Mom found a church she liked and took us kids to Sunday services. Dad was fine with it, even supportive, since he was raised as a secular Jew, rather than in an observant Jewish home.

When I was nine, my father placed a twenty-dollar Sears and Roebuck Silvertone guitar in my hands, and my love affair with music officially began. By the time I was in junior high, I had my own little rock band. In high school, I wrote music and made money playing gigs. I even sang on demo records in New York City studios. I chose to attend Baldwin Wallace College—a small, private liberal arts school just outside Cleveland, Ohio—because of its highly rated music conservatory and family feel.

At Baldwin Wallace, the music majors didn't select the teacher they wanted; rather, the teachers listened to them audition and then selected the students they preferred for their private studios. The instructor who chose me was Professor Charles H. Smith, the cantor of a prestigious Reform synagogue in downtown Cleveland simply called "the Temple." So instead of partying with my fraternity brothers every Friday night, I could be found sitting next to Cantor Smith in the choir loft of the Temple, singing Hebrew prayers and perfecting my vocal technique.

It wasn't long before my musical aspirations changed from rock and pop to opera and sacred Jewish music. Soon Cantor Smith introduced me to the recordings of Richard Tucker, an amazing operatic tenor and a religious Jew. I had a new hero in my life. I would endeavor to emulate his career and life for years to come.

After graduating from college, I headed home for a few months to work double shifts in one of my dad's client's paper mills. The workplace was unbearably hot, extremely dangerous, and completely exhausting, but I found the union scale pay irresistible. After surviving three months at the mill, I finally earned enough money to pack a small steamer trunk and head to Milan, Italy, to continue my education in singing and opera.

I only had a few problems. I spoke no Italian, had no contacts in Milan, and had no idea where I would live. But if opera is what you want to sing, where better to learn it than La Scala opera house in

Milan? A hundred dollars purchased me a ride across the Atlantic Ocean in the belly of the *Michelangelo*, an Italian luxury liner. I eventually found a bedroom for rent in a small Italian apartment occupied by an elderly woman and her fifty-six-year-old son. My accommodations included a windowsill for my cold food storage and a washboard in the tub, where I was permitted to bathe and do laundry with hot water three times each week. Looking back, I am still amazed at the great lengths I went to in furthering my career, but passionately pursuing my goals would soon become the trademark of my life and ministry.

I secured a spot in the studio of a highly esteemed voice teacher, Señora Guarini. With some private lessons in the Italian language, I was up and running. However, after only six months of this adventurous student lifestyle, I returned to Cleveland to try to make a living.

I landed jobs at two high schools teaching guitar and vocal classes. Every morning at 7:30 a.m. I was greeted by thirty eager young teenagers with untuned guitars and untrained fingers. I survived two years of that schedule, traveling each day between the two large high schools of the district before finally calling it quits to pursue my chosen career as a cantor and opera singer.

I was told Indiana University had the finest music program in the world. Many of its graduate students went on to wonderful careers as artists and teachers. Apparently, my audition in the summer of 1976 went well enough, because the next thing I knew, I was driving my 1968 Chevy Bel Air to Bloomington, Indiana. With a room in the graduate dorm, a wonderful voice teacher, and a part-time job with the university, I was back in the saddle, riding briskly into the future I had planned for myself.

Life was good—until my attractive accompanist, a Baptist girl from Georgia, asked me to go to church with her. Church was not unfamiliar to me, given that my mother had taken me there regularly when I was young, but it was never my first or even last choice for a date. My lifestyle and attitude reflected that of my peers of the 1960s, so I held a very low opinion of the church, its message, and especially the quality of its music. But something happened that Sunday morning that would change my life forever.

I knew fairly well what to expect. A podium stood in the middle of the stage with a small choir standing on risers around it. Three numbers posted on either side of the stage corresponded to the page numbers of the hymnal in the seat pocket in front of me—those would be the ones we would sing. *Yup, just as I expected.* Next, the minister would welcome us all to stand and sing all fifteen verses of the first song—*but wait, what's this?*

A young man started the service with a song and a guitar. *Well, at least this is different.* Jerry Williams, a guest from Florida, had come to interview for the position of youth pastor in this fledgling independent church which had recently separated from its liberal-leaning Presbyterian roots of many years.

Two things were immediately obvious to me when "Brother Jerry" opened his mouth. First, his West Texas twang revealed he wasn't from anywhere near Florida. Second, he seemed to actually know the God he was singing to. When he sang, I began to feel something going on in the atmosphere around me. What it was, I had no idea—maybe someone was playing with the air conditioning? I remember turning to my friend and saying, "If they don't hire that guy who sang, they're nuts."

The experience with that simple song intrigued me. I found myself going back to the church again and again on Sunday nights, hoping to experience the same feeling I'd had when the guy from Texas sang, but he never reappeared. I asked several times what had happened to the young man from Florida, who I knew really had to be from Texas, but no one seemed to know what I was talking about.

Several weeks later, I received a call from the church secretary, who told me I had been invited by an anonymous church family to come for a meal on the following Sunday night. Free food? As a starving grad student on a tight budget, I immediately accepted. When I arrived at the address I'd been given, I was surprised to see it was an apartment building. When the door opened, you could have knocked me over with a feather. Standing in the doorway was "Brother Jerry."

"Come on in, bruhtha," he said with a huge Texan smile.

A few weeks later, Jerry invited me on a fishing trip in Tennessee. There, I heard his life story and personal testimony. As I listened intently, I realized that I needed to know God. Jerry told me of his years of sinful, wild living and how Jesus had completely changed his life, forgiven him, and sent him out to help others just like him. Little did he know that he was describing my own life. Not only that, but I desperately wanted to be reconciled to the God I sang about in the Temple choir loft.

The next morning, I awoke with a new hope in my heart. I got up extra early and decided to take a walk down by the river. As I walked, with the sun just peeking through the tall trees and birds beginning their day in song, I felt it again—that same feeling of the atmosphere changing around me. At first it felt spooky, like someone might be watching me from behind one of the massive water oaks. But then it felt peaceful, identical to how it had felt that day at church. I stopped walking, sat down on an old tree stump, and began praying.

"I have sung about You, but I don't know You," I said. "I've made a mess of my life, but now I am giving it to You. Amen."

When I finally stood up, somehow I knew I was forgiven. Strange thoughts washed over my mind, like "God loves me. I'm forgiven." A huge weight lifted off my heart and mind, and I knew I belonged to God.

A TIME FOR HARVEST

Jerry and I started singing together the original songs he had written. Next, we added my buddy Ed Kerr, and that same strange change in the atmosphere happened every time we sang together. Before we knew it, Zondervan Corporation called, and we began making records for them as a gospel singing group called Harvest.

We spent five amazing years together, making records and sharing our love for God. In that time, my love for Jesus grew by leaps and bounds as I worked a full-time job, finished graduate school, traveled full-time, and made records with Harvest. I married the prettiest girl at church (not my accompanist), had our first son, and tried to write music that our band of brothers could record. The only problem was that everything I wrote sounded like it belonged in a synagogue, not a church.

I spent most of my time in the Bible reading the Psalms and the books written by the prophets of Israel. Of course, I read and memorized lots of New Covenant verses as well, but my Jewish soul found great comfort and inspiration in those Old Testament writings.

On a ministry trip with Harvest in the summer of 1980, Jerry pointed out a poster hanging in a church lobby about a Messianic Jewish singing group called Lamb. Next, someone at a church somewhere handed me a cassette tape from a Jewish believer named Sid Roth. He had a radio program called *Messianic Vision* and interviewed Jewish people who had found their Messiah. *What? There are more of us out there?*

Soon I found myself listening to testimonies of other Jewish believers on cassette tapes and reading pamphlets about their experiences with God. As I listened to the tapes and read their stories, I couldn't stop crying. I wasn't really sure why, but I knew I had to be around other Jewish believers who loved our people enough to speak the truth about our Messiah in love.

After a brief phone conversation with Sid Roth, my wife and I borrowed a car that could actually make the journey from Bloomington, Indiana, to Rockville, Maryland, and back in four days. We met with Sid, attended a Friday night Shabbat service at his Messianic synagogue, and drove back to Indiana in time for the next Harvest engagement. After much prayer and anguishing over the decision, my wife and I knew we had to leave Harvest and invest our lives in that little Messianic synagogue called Beth Messiah.

We said our prayerful and tearful goodbyes and headed to Maryland. We had no place to live, no jobs, and found ourselves in a very expensive area just outside Washington, D.C.

But God! Within a week, I had two jobs, a lovely townhouse to rent, and I was the new cantor at Beth Messiah. We offered more contemporary services on Friday evenings and a Torah service on Saturday mornings. Before long, I had formed a new traveling singing group we called Israel's Hope. Now every song I wrote fit into the warp and woof of our Messianic Jewish worship and praise. Soon Maranatha! Music invited us to make records with them.

We put down some roots for the next ten years, singing and traveling with two other Messianic Jewish brothers in the Lord. Finally, it was time to move again, this time to Chicago to serve as the worship leader and associate pastor at a large independent evangelical church in the far-south suburbs. Our plans included my leading a Friday night Messianic service at the church while performing my regular duties and establishing a new pattern for successful Messianic church planting. However, soon after we arrived, the pastor decided that housing two separate communities in the same space wasn't what he wanted to do after all, so that dream would have to wait a few more years.

The blow was softened a bit when Integrity Music called. I made the first Messianic Jewish record with Integrity Music right there at the church in the fall of 1990.

BORN TO DO THIS

Four years after that one-time project, Integrity Music called again. I had been wondering what had happened to my dreams of being a cantor who knew the God of Israel and who would sing the songs of Zion's King to our Jewish people. I longed to be a voice that would cause the heart of the Church to turn again to Jerusalem and to love our Jewish people, who so desperately need to know our Messiah. When my phone rang that fall day in 1994, all my questions vanished after only two minutes on the phone with Don Moen.

Don, a well-known worship artist, and Michael Coleman, the founder and CEO of Integrity Music, had been at a conference where Pastor Jack Hayford was speaking on the Psalms of Ascent. These were the songs of King David (Psalms 120–134) that the children of Israel would use as they ascended the mountains of Judea to come before the Lord three times each year for the major feasts—Passover, Pentecost, and Tabernacles. As Don and Mike sat listening to Pastor Jack speak that day, they both found themselves thinking the same thing: *We need*

to go to Jerusalem during one of these feasts and record a live project using
these Psalms of David. But who should we get to do this recording?

"Paul, Mike and I are here in California with Pastor Jack," Don
said, "and we would like you to consider coming to Jerusalem with
us to produce a live recording during Passover next year. What do
you think?"

Before I could collect my thoughts, I blurted out, "Don, I was born
to do this project."

Within six months, my wife and I said our goodbyes to Chicago
and headed to Jerusalem to capture the first live Messianic Jewish
recording in the International Convention Center. The event would
come to be known as "Shalom Jerusalem." Three years later, the *Shalom Jerusalem* album had sold more than a million copies worldwide
and would later be recorded in Spanish and Portuguese.

We returned to Jerusalem in 1998 for another record titled *Jerusalem Arise*. This too would produce amazing results, as we introduced "Days of Elijah," the very popular song by Robin Mark. Many
more records would follow these in my twenty-seven-year association
with Integrity. We traveled to seventy-five nations, recorded in five
languages, and saw many Jews and Gentiles receive the life-changing
message of Yeshua—Jesus the Messiah.

And so it was that I found myself at that stage of my story after
wrapping up my time with Integrity and wrestling with the "Blackbird" God wanted me to build.

THE BLACKBIRD SOARS

Now that I had the plan for the Blackbird, I had a new problem:
I am only one man. A plane needs an entire team to take off. I simply

could not get that colossal mission underway alone. Once I had clarity about the *where, what,* and *how,* I needed the *who.*

I was going to need some major *whos* to walk this thing out with me. This Blackbird would need some expert design and crafting right from its inception. I also would need a venue, a camera crew, equipment, a sound crew, technical crew, hosting, advertising, coordination, hotel, food, transportation—plus a dedicated staff that could spend a good fourteen months working on all these details. And, oh yes—we would need to write the songs that would give our Blackbird wings to fly.

If I told you that I wasn't the least bit intimidated by all this, I'd be flat-out lying. But the passion for the vision I had heard and seen that day in my quiet-time chair got my feet on the floor every morning in faith that it would somehow become a reality by God's grace.

I soon found myself on the phone sharing the vision and looking for people to partner with me to hear the Lion of Judah roar. To my great surprise and delight, none of those early calls were turned down. GOD TV said *yes* to filming and broadcasting the event; the International Christian Embassy Jerusalem said *yes* to securing the large venue in the city; Sar-El Tours said *yes* to coordinating a large tour, along with other groups. TBN's studio in Jerusalem said *yes* to filming a second concert there. CBN said *yes* to helping with video production.

Every player, worship leader, and singer I called gave a very quick and decided *yes* to my invitation to Jerusalem. Some even said, "Don't worry about paying me—just cover my expenses and I am good to go." Before long, I had an amazing group of anointed worshipers consisting of Arab Christians, Messianic Jews, and Christian Zionists from around the globe who would create the sound to provoke a *sha'ag* from Heaven.

Amazing. And just like that, the opening song seemed to roll off our tongues in the basement of the Brownstone Recording Studio in Nashville, Tennessee:

Roar from Zion, one Nation, one King,
People of God, say
Roar from Zion, from the east, from the west,
To worship your holiness.
Rejoice all you nations, hear me O Israel,
Yeshua has triumphed, His Kingdom is over all.
Prisoners of hope, be now restored,
The Lion of Judah is raising His sword.
The King is among us, Shepherd of Righteousness,
He's gathered His people, called them to holiness.
His presence returned, the veil has been torn,
The glory departed has now been restored.
Baruch haba, b'shem Adonai
Blessed is He who comes in the name of the Lord.
Roar from Zion, *Mashiach Yeshua*, Lion of Judah
Roar from Zion, the sound of Your voice
Thunders from Jerusalem.[1]

Now all I had to do was write the rest of the songs, produce the music, and raise a couple hundred thousand dollars. I met with Paul Mills, one of Nashville's leading Christian orchestrators, and tasked him with setting the entire opening video with a dramatic string orchestra. CBN assigned a top video producer to turn all the music

---

1 Paul Wilbur and Dan Needham, "Roar from Zion," RFZ Media, 2017.

and scripture into a dynamic video that would serve as a runway to give the Roar some room to take off.

We were getting closer to putting wings on the Blackbird. But what about the rest of the music? Joshua Aaron provided an anointed declaration from Joshua 24. Jamie Hilsden from Jerusalem wrote a wonderful chorus out of Psalm 44:8. Sarah Liberman extended her amazing praise with "Gadol Adonai" (Great Is the Lord). My daughter-in-law Shae Wilbur wrote and performed her new song "Endless." Ryan and Marie Hodges brought their original song of victory, "O We Praise the Name."

The other songs needed to tell the story came in time, many of them collaborations with me and my producer, Dan Needham: "The King Is Coming," "Song of Victory," and "It Is Good to Praise the Lord." We added the well-known songs "Adonai," "Even So," and an updated version of "Days of Elijah."

We were almost ready to head to Jerusalem. Only one question remained: *Where would we get all the shekels needed to pay the bills?*

EVERY VISION HAS A COST

In the Gospel of Luke, we read about just such a situation: "But don't begin until you count the cost. For who would begin construction of a building without first calculating the cost to see if there is enough money to finish it?" Nobody wants to be part of a half-baked project. So out came the pencil, the paper, and the calculator. The budget to build this "Blackbird," even while calling in favors from friends, was just shy of $200,000.

What did we have in hand to get the ball rolling, with the recording date only nine months away? About $15,000. As it drew nearer, the budget grew to $250,000 and our account still had only $25,000—but we did sense some signs that God was at work. While traveling and ministering in the Netherlands, our hosts handed us an additional $15,000 toward the recording budget. Then one of our board members wrote a check for $10,000 and promised to solicit others for more. Very encouraging, but we were still a long way from where we needed to be.

Then, all of a sudden, Heaven broke loose.

On our last night in Amsterdam, I was preparing to travel to Jerusalem for more ministry when my phone lit up around 1:00 a.m. It was my son Joel, calling and texting from Los Angeles. I was so tired I almost ignored the calls and texts, but then I thought, *Joel never does this unless it's very important.* So I called him back and sat down on my bed, ready to fall, exhausted, into the comfortable covers. When he answered, I warned him, "I am super tired and on my way to Jerusalem in just a few hours."

"Okay, Dad, I'll make this quick," he said. "What if I told you I am holding a check for $25,000 dollars for the new project in my hands?"

There was a long pause from me.

"Praise the Lord! What a great surprise!" I finally responded, suddenly more awake. "Where did it come from?"

"So you're saying it's good that I called?" he asked. "Then what if I told you that it was for $50,000 dollars? Would that be even better?"

I began to wonder if my second-born was just having some fun at my expense.

"Joel, if this is a joke, I will spank you like a three-year-old at Toys 'R' Us," I said, halfway meaning it.

"Well, okay, then, sit down," he replied. "I know this check is good because I know where it came from. I'm holding a check for $100,000 dollars to help pay for the new CD/DVD launch of Wilbur Ministries."

Isn't it amazing how quickly good news can energize even the weariest soul? Faith comes by hearing—and my faith had just taken a huge leap forward. I knew then that YHVH had taken up this cause, and He would see it through to the end.

That gift came from Japan, of all places. It turned out that a package of our CDs and books had been sent to someone in England who had ordered from our online store. Somehow, the package never made it to England, but was delivered instead to an address in Japan. We looked into the error and discovered the Japanese address belonged to an American Messianic Jew who was married to a Japanese man. (Seriously, you just can't make this stuff up.) As a result of the redirected package, this lady became a friend of our ministry. When she heard about the live recording, she sat down and wrote that incredible check. Our Father truly works in mysterious and amazing ways.

A few weeks later, I was on a call with a large corporation that was considering investing in the project with plans for reimbursement once it was finished. Two attorneys on the call were trying to work out the legal bugs of the deal. After months of discussions and now several hours on this call, my corporate-leader friend said, "Guys, I just don't see how this deal can ever work..."

My heart sank.

"...so I have decided to simply give the funds as a gift," he concluded.

I can't tell you for certain that I ever heard an angel before that moment, but I know I heard one that day. Both lawyers fell absolutely silent, and quite frankly, I was left bumbling and stumbling for words of gratitude and thanks that I am certain fell woefully short of what I was feeling. God is truly good, and His steadfast love endures forever.

We had the funds, the team, and the blueprints for our Blackbird. Everything for the performance was set. All that remained was for God to use the coming Roar to reunite His people. After all, how hard could it possibly be to unite Jews and Gentiles, to hear the Church and Israel singing the same songs of Zion to the same King?

CHAPTER 3

A HOUSE DIVIDED

Anyone who knows anything about the history of God's people knows that uniting Jews and Gentiles has never been an easy task. Some might even call it impossible. Yet that is exactly what Jesus came to do—to draw all people to the one true God through Him, with both the Jews and the rest of the world being "grafted in," as the Apostle Paul described it in his letter to the Romans.

We are called to fulfill an assignment similar to the one the King gave those first-century disciples. If you recall, they once asked Yeshua (Jesus) that question recorded in Acts 1:6 (ESV): "Lord, will you at this time restore the kingdom to Israel?" There are hundreds, if not thousands, of verses that speak of the restoration of Israel, which is a kind of priesthood among the nations. The reason for this, I believe, is that the Sovereign Lord fully intends to have what He wants: His Kingdom on Earth as it is in Heaven. To do that, He must have a people, a land, and a king. He is the King, and He is reacquiring the land and restoring the people.

> In that day I will restore David's fallen shelter—
> I will repair its broken walls and restore its ruins—
> and will rebuild it as it used to be.... (Amos 9:11 NIV)

> At that time I will gather you;
> At that time I will bring you home.
> I will give you honor and praise
> among all the peoples of the earth
> when I restore your fortunes before your very eyes. (Zephaniah 3:20 NIV)

These are pretty bold statements given to a small nation all those centuries ago. Apart from the intervention of some superhero, they seem to be just the hopeful musings of a desert priest, poet, or prophet. And yet it doesn't take a rocket scientist to see that much of what many considered "impossible" is already well underway.

Against all odds, the modern nation of Israel arose from the ashes of the Holocaust in 1948 and was voted into existence by a very reluctant gathering of the newly formed United Nations. The horrors of the Holocaust momentarily shocked the collective conscience of the world long enough to move the debate in favor of the devastated Jewry for a brief moment in history. If that same vote were taken today, the resolution for an independent Jewish state would go down in flames. Militant Islamism, white supremacy, and antisemitism have now risen to levels not seen since the genocide of the 1930s—not to mention an entire movement that aims to boycott Israeli goods, force people to divest of their investments in Israel, and punish nations that don't comply.

Sadly, ignorant church doctrines like replacement theology and supersessionism have done much harm. These two similar ideologies essentially say that all of God's promises to ethnic Israel now apply to the Church instead, yet all the curses on ethnic Israel still apply to the Jews. Even some of the most revered voices of the Church, beginning as early as the second century, excluded the Jewish people from various promises given to Abraham in Genesis and took them for themselves. But those prophecies of blessing were not given to a people who thought they deserved them. Rather, they were given to a scattered, chased, hunted, hated, and nationally disenfranchised people, so that when the promises were fulfilled, the nations would be stunned into realizing that only the God of Israel could do such things.

Ever since the miracle of 1948, when David Ben-Gurion announced the rebirth of the independent State of Israel to the entire world, the tiny Jewish nation has had to defend itself to the death many times without the help of any "Christian" nations. Immediately following this announcement, seven Arab nations united to attack the fledgling nation with the intent of killing the Jews and wiping the memory of Israel from the face of the earth. They failed.

In 1967, Jerusalem, which was established some three thousand years previously as Israel's capital by King David, was finally restored as one undivided city. To this day, Israelis consider Jerusalem to be the beloved and eternal capital of the State of Israel. But this great event came at the expense of the Six-Day War, which cost more than twenty thousand Arab and eight hundred Israeli lives. Make no mistake about who was and is the ultimate victor here: "He who keepeth Israel neither slumbers, nor sleeps" (Psalm 121:4 KJV).

These events only go to show the infallible truth: the Lion of Judah never fails. As the Prophet Balaam rightly declared in Numbers 23:19 (NIV):

> God is not a man, that He should lie,
> Not a son of man that He should change His mind.
> Does He speak and then not act?
> Does He promise and not fulfill?
> I have received a command to bless;
> He has blessed, and I cannot change it.

Twenty-five years later, five Arab nations, under the direction of Egypt, pulled off a surprise attack while most of Israel's Jews were fasting and praying during the holiest day of the year, resulting in the Yom Kippur War of 1973. It was a brilliant plan that nearly cost the Israelis their nation, had it not been for aid sent by U.S. President Richard Nixon.

A CHRISTIAN BLOCKADE

Trust me when I say that all the Jewish people remember the Christian "witness" of the past with the pogroms of Russia, the Spanish Inquisition, the death marches in Ukraine, the virulent antisemitism of some Church fathers, and the Nazi Holocaust. In the Jewish mind, all these atrocities were done in the name of Christianity—or at least by people who thought they were Christians. The Jewish people cannot help but see flashes of these horrors when they think of the Gentiles' Messiah. Yes, there are a few trees planted on the grounds of Yad Vashem in Jerusalem to honor the memory of "Righteous Gentiles" like Corrie ten Boom and Oskar Schindler, who placed their lives on the line to rescue Jews during World War II, but there should be thousands of those names—not merely dozens.

This conflict between Jews and Gentiles did not stop in Israel. I have come into contact with this polarizing attitude between the twin kingdoms of Christianity and Judaism many times throughout my life as a Messianic Jew for a couple reasons. First, the reality is that there is endemic and historic antisemitism in the nations and, sadly, in the Church. Second, there has been a "blindness in part" regarding the Gospel among our Jewish people that was imposed by Heaven. (See Romans 11:25.)

It has seemed impossible to move these two Kingdom mountains closer together or to penetrate their well-fortified walls and defenses. Unfortunately, the perceived actions (and sometimes the inactions) of the Church have done very little to even suggest to the Jewish people that Jesus of Nazareth is indeed the Messiah of Israel. I am not trying to be critical here, just simply stating a fact. Thus, there remains an insular resistance to the message of the prophets and the entire scope of the Scriptures, frustrating the messengers of hope and salvation to Israel, both Jew and Gentile.

Christian antisemitism is one blockade to conquer. It is stubborn to root out and difficult to understand. The ugly and mostly untold story is well documented in Dr. Michael L. Brown's classic work *Our Hands Are Stained with Blood* (Destiny Image, 1992). I truly wish I had encountered this work before my first unscheduled public debate with an Orthodox rabbi.

My unplanned encounter with this dark side of church history took place on the very Jewish campus of American University in the heart of Washington, D.C., in 1982. I was manning the Messianic materials outreach table one day, and everything was going reasonably well—until I was approached by an Orthodox rabbi from the local Chabad house. He listened intently as I shared with students who stopped at the table to see what I had to give away. Whenever a Jewish student looked interested, he simply told them, "This stuff isn't for you," and they would walk away.

Of course, the truth was that this "stuff" was exactly for them. After a little more time passed, the rabbi felt comfortable enough to come sit beside me and engage in some small talk. He continued to shoo the Jewish students away from the table from time to time. I noticed a small audience began to form as the questions he posed became more personal and pointed. I was well-equipped to counter them with my list of prophecies and promises fulfilled by God. After all, being a Jew myself brought with it certain opportunities to share my faith with close family and friends.

But this rabbi was different. He knew all the verses I offered as proof of Yeshua's Messiahship and quickly took a different tack. "So, tell me your testimony of how you came to believe in Jesus Christ," he asked.

"You mean Yeshua HaMashiach?" I jumped at the chance. "Why, of course!" The crowd continued to grow, and people listened intently, with some Christian students adding a few sounds of approval during my story of faith. Suddenly, the rabbi interrupted me with some pointed questions.

"Is this faith for Jews too, or only for Gentiles?" I answered easily with Romans 1:16–17, saying that this Gospel was first for the Jew, but also for the Gentile. I spoke about the one true olive tree of God and how being a part of this tree has brought peace and love for both groups. I shared that one of Jesus's names is *Sar Shalom*, Prince of Peace.

"So," the rabbi interjected, "anyone who loves your Jesus would certainly love the Jewish people because they have this new heart of love and peace, right?"

"Of course, right." I smiled as I answered the question.

He responded simply, "So, tell me who said to 'burn all the Jewish books, forbid them to teach or pray, don't sell to them or buy from them,' then broke down their houses and synagogues and treated them like dogs, and more?"

A quiet hush fell in the hall as people waited for my answer.

"Why, Hitler, of course, or someone like him?" I answered with a bit of a question in my voice.

The rabbi sat back and concluded, "Martin Luther, your great German reformer and lover of your Jesus Christ, said that and much more. He even wrote a famous book titled *On the Jews and Their Lies*. Hitler did say these things and more, but he was only quoting your Martin Luther."

I sat there in stunned silence. I didn't know what to say, but I felt in my gut that he was telling me and all those listening the sad and unthinkable truth. My heart sank.

I felt like I had just been sucker-punched by someone who knew how to hit hard. I simply gathered my things, got up from the table, and left campus with tears running down my face. I felt betrayed, even abandoned. The faith that had brought me such joy and confidence was now being busted up with the sledgehammers of fear, doubt, and unbelief. *Have I believed a lie? How can this be true?*

All this and much more haunted me for several weeks. I went home and told my wife what had happened. She had grown up in a loving Presbyterian church with her family in Bloomington, Indiana, and had never heard these things either. As we prayed together, I asked her to give me some time to work out my thoughts. I wasn't quite sure where I would land at the end of the day.

Thankfully, I had the good counsel and friendship of other Jewish believers like Sid Roth, Dan Juster, Keith Intrater, and Andrew Shishkoff to help me work through the fallout of that information overload. After several weeks of prayer and fasting, I reconciled what I had learned with the truth of God's Word and emerged from those dark woods.

Unfortunately, a young man who shared duties with me at the outreach table didn't fare quite as well. He went to a Shabbat dinner at the rabbi's house and never returned to worship with us again. In fact, he turned up years later as one of the region's best-known leaders in the new anti-missionary group called Jews for Judaism. He earned a law degree and became a formidable sparring partner in the two-thousand-year-old debate, "Is Yeshua the Messiah of Israel?"

THE TRUTH ABOUT YESHUA

Another huge blockade to the truth about Yeshua is that the rabbis and generations of fathers have taught children that the "Jesus of the Gentiles is not for us." My friend and mentor Sid Roth, host of *It's Supernatural* and president of the Messianic Vision ministry, told me of a time when, as a young Jewish professional working in a prestigious brokerage firm in downtown Washington, D.C., he was approached by a zealous Christian coworker who shared the Gospel with him. Not quite thirty years old at the time, Sid was totally offended by this young man, but not for the reason you might think: Sid couldn't believe this coworker thought he was gullible enough to believe that Jesus Christ of the Gentiles was actually a Jewish rabbi born in Israel!

Still fuming at the end of the day, Sid went home and told his Orthodox Jewish mother about the exquisite ruse his coworker had tried to pull on him. But instead of a consoling rebuttal to his friend's assertion, she said that the Christian man had actually told him the truth. It didn't take long for Sid to examine the facts for himself, and then become one of the boldest witnesses for Israel's Messiah that I have ever known.

But the rabbis tell us Jesus was deceived. By declaring that He was the Messiah, they tell us, He led many astray in His day. He taught lots of good things and did some miracles, but then He was crucified by the Romans. His disciples stole His body and tried to convince people that He had been raised from the dead. His disciples also took the life and times of Jesus and looked for passages of the Scriptures that might suggest He somehow was walking out what had been prophesied many centuries earlier—but those verses were not speaking about a messiah at all. We are told that one great proof that Jesus wasn't the Messiah is that we Jews have not believed in Him or followed Him for two thousand years. And many of the Gentiles who worship Him have done nothing but persecute and slaughter us that entire time.

So how did Sid and so many others overcome this mountain that blocks the path of truth for any Jew in any generation? Only by the grace of God. As the Apostle Paul put it, "For I am not ashamed of the gospel, because it is the power of God that brings salvation to everyone who believes: first to the Jew, then to the Gentile. For in the gospel the righteousness of God is revealed—a righteousness that is by faith from first to last, just as it is written: 'The righteous will live by faith'" (Romans 1:16 NIV).

Every Jew has that message from the rabbis playing in their heads when they hear the name of Jesus. Some thoughtful Jewish scholars have even come to the conclusion after much investigation that Jesus must be the Messiah for the Gentiles because of His life and impact— but He simply cannot be the Messiah of Israel. The Holy One of Israel, the *Ruach HaKodesh*, the Holy Spirit is the only One who can shut off the taped program and turn on the light of truth in any heart. Pray that now is the time to turn on the Light of Life.

OPPORTUNITY FOR CHANGE

When the righteous deeds of Christians are irrefutably linked with the name of Jesus the Messiah, then Jerusalem will have the witness to cause her to declare, "Blessed is He who comes in the name of the Lord." So if our Blackbird is to soar and bring hope to Israel and the nations, things will need to change. All these years I have hoped that our music would gain a unique opportunity to change the reputation of Jesus in the hearts and minds of our own Jewish people. In the words of the Messiah:

> If a kingdom is divided against itself, that kingdom cannot stand. If a house is divided against itself, that house cannot stand. (Mark 3: 24–25 NIV)

Up to this point in history, the Kingdom of God and the demonstration of the One New Man has been hard to find at best and torn apart at worst. The time has come for us as followers of Jesus the Messiah to lay down our swords and take up a spirit of humility and serve our Jewish brothers and sisters in love.

SECTION 2

DEMONSTRATION
OF THE SPIRIT

CHAPTER 4

THE DAY JESUS
CAME TO CHURCH

For the revelation awaits an appointed time; it speaks
of the end and will not prove false.
—*Habakkuk 2:3 NIV*

Month after month and year after year, we held Shabbat services at our home church in Jacksonville, Florida (Celebration Church), called First Friday. We invited the whole city to join us for an evening of worship and teaching, hoping to draw out a curious Jewish community. Some did come, but mostly we ministered to a Gentile Christian Zionist audience.

"What will it take to penetrate the centuries of antisemitism, bad teaching and doctrine, and just plain stony hearts on both sides of this 'middle wall of partition' that the blood of the Lamb of God has broken down?" I often asked myself and the Lord.

And then in March 2018, something remarkable happened in Jacksonville that would literally change our lives forever and help me understand what the Roar and Thunder God had tasked me with creating were all about.

Celebration Church is a large, independent, charismatic church with many campuses throughout the city and around the world. The founders and senior pastors, Stovall and Kerri Weems, planted it with a few friends in 1998. They began with hopes, dreams, and a word from God to plant a local assembly that would make a difference in these last days. Although I didn't have any connection with Celebration at that time, that was when I moved from Colorado Springs to Jacksonville with a word from God to reunite my family, who had been scattered all over the map.

By 2018, even though we were very involved with Celebration Church and had led a Shabbat service there each month for years, we were not part of the staff. So when I was invited to preach the Good Friday service that March, it was an unexpected honor. I really wanted to accept and felt led to do it. The only problem was that I had already made solid commitments to other pastors for that special weekend.

As I prayed over the dilemma, I heard the Lord say, "Call your friends, tell them the situation, and ask them to release you. If they do, remain and preach the service here, but if not, go and fulfill your promise to them." So that is exactly what I did. When my friends in Chicago and Dallas heard my heart on the matter, they graciously released me to remain in Jacksonville. I wasn't exactly sure why, but I believed I was supposed to be there for that service.

I didn't realize the importance of that particular Good Friday until I opened my calendar and discovered it was also the first night of Passover. *Aha*, I thought, *now I get it*. I decided the message would be about how Jesus fulfilled God's ancient promise to Abraham when He provided a lamb in place of Isaac in Genesis 22, and then for the whole world in Luke 22. *Yes.* After I showed them the pattern and promise in the Passover Seder meal, we would serve the people communion so they could make a covenant with YHVH in the body and blood of His Son, Yeshua. *This will be powerful.*

I began to plan exactly what I could share in my allotted twenty-two minutes. I knew the mysteries revealed in the Passover would really bless our congregation, but I was not prepared for the blessings that would be released in my own life.

On Friday, March 30, 2018, my world changed forever. I call it the Day Jesus Came to Church. It gave a whole new meaning and understanding of what Peter preached in Jerusalem: "For He [Jesus] must remain in heaven until the time for the final restoration of all things, as God promised long ago through his holy prophets" (Acts 3:21 NIV).

I believe a new *time* began that day—a time that will take us to the culmination of all things with the return of Jesus the Messiah to sit on His throne in Jerusalem. For on that day, I heard the Lion of the Tribe of Judah ROAR.

THE SERVICE

As I mentioned, Good Friday was also the first night of Passover in 2018. The two calendars of the Bible and Pope Gregory were on a parallel course with what I now believe was a Heaven-directed outcome. All 3,400 seats in the sanctuary at Celebration Church were filled, with some people having to stand behind the last rows and wishing they had come a bit earlier. The worship team did a wonderful job leading us in song and pointing our hearts toward Heaven to the sacrifice of the Lamb of God.

After a few announcements and a video, it was my turn to speak. Because of the time limitations, I only brought the most important items for my message about the Passover Seder meal—the matzo and the cup. I would only be able to mention the rest of the traditional elements.

I explained that the night was special not only because it was Good Friday, a few days prior to Resurrection Sunday, but also because it was the first night of Passover, which precedes the Feast of First Fruits. That was the celebration taking place at the time of the death and resurrection of Jesus the Messiah, as described in the gospels and by the Apostle Paul (Matthew 28, Mark 16, Luke 24, John 20, and 1 Corinthians 15).

I turned first to the four promises God had given through Moses to the enslaved Israelites in Exodus 6:6–7:

> Therefore, say to the Israelites; "I am the Lord, and I will bring you out from under the yoke of the Egyptians. I will free you from being slaves to them, and I will redeem you with an outstretched arm and with mighty acts of judgment. I will take you as my own people, and I will be your God." (NIV)

Each of these promises is represented by a cup of wine, sipped at intervals throughout the Passover meal. The meal itself tells the story of the Israelites' deliverance after more than four hundred years of slavery in Egypt.

Each cup appearing during the Seder meal has a unique purpose and name based on the promise it represents. For instance, the first cup is called "Sanctification" and comes at the beginning of the meal. It corresponds to the first promise of God to "bring them out" or sanctify the Israelites. The second is the "Cup of Plagues." It is not consumed, but rather poured out in remembrance of the judgments that fell on the Egyptians for worshiping false gods. The third cup comes right after dinner, just as described in Luke 22, and is called the "Cup of Redemption." The fourth and final cup is the "Cup of Praise," or the "Hallel Cup," and is shared at the close of the covenant meal.

I intended to move rather quickly through the telling of the story of the original Exodus and then retell it through the gospel accounts of the Last Supper, where Yeshua initiated the promised New Covenant in His own body and blood as the sacrificial Lamb of God who takes away the sins of the world, as His cousin John had prophesied three years before at His baptism in the Jordan River. As He initiated this New Covenant, the cup and bread became much more than reminders of an ancient deliverance; rather, they became the body and blood of the Lamb of God, the New Covenant that would redeem Israel and the entire world.

Just as the four cups of wine have their place and special names, the bread (or matzo) also has a place of honor at this meal. During Passover we use unleavened bread, also called "the bread of affliction," for several reasons. We are told in Leviticus 23 not to eat leavened bread during this feast or for seven more days as part of the Feast of Unleavened Bread. The Apostle Paul reminds us that leaven, or yeast, is often a symbol of sin. Just as the yeast puffs up the bread, so pride can puff us up and bring with it "every evil thing" (1 Corinthians 5:6).

The matzo also has other symbolic attributes that are significant for the believer in Jesus: It is bruised, striped, and pierced. The Prophet Isaiah describes it in detail in his most famous Chapter 53. It is plain and unattractive, usually rejected by folks during the rest of the year for its lack of flavor. It is bruised by its contact with the oven. It is striped by the pressure and design of the baker and finally pierced many times to speed up the baking process.

Lots of matzo is brought to the table for use during the Passover celebration, but there is also a separate grouping of matzo used for a particular purpose. A special three-compartment bag called a *matzo tash* (Yiddish for "matzo bag") containing three sheets of matzo is placed on the table. During the early portion of the meal, the middle loaf is removed from the other two and broken in half with blessings proclaimed over it. Half remains on the table while the other half is wrapped in a white linen cloth and hidden away (symbolically buried), before returning at the end of the feast. The wrapped portion is given a new name, *Afikomen*, which means, "I will come again." It reappears after dinner during the telling of the Passover story. This special bread must be purchased back (or redeemed) to the table with pieces of silver paid to the child who finds the "burial place" in the house.

The symbolism here is just as striking as the names of the cups of wine. I love hearing people's responses when they hear the deep mysteries revealed by the Passover meal. The picture painted could not be any clearer for those who have eyes to see.

As I prepared to distribute the broken bread and the wine of the third cup during my message, I called Pastor Stovall Weems to join me on the platform so we could serve our church family the New Covenant meal of our Messiah's body and blood—the Lord's Supper.

And that's when everything changed.

THE ENCOUNTER

As Pastor Stovall joined me, I reached for the special matzo set aside in the linen cloth. I unwrapped it while quoting from Luke 22:19:

"And he took bread, gave thanks and broke it, and gave it to them, saying, 'This is my body given for you; do this in remembrance of me'" (NIV).

I handed Pastor Stovall a piece of the *Afikomen* and spoke the traditional Hebrew blessing: *"Baruch atah Adonai, Eloheinu melech ha olam, hamotzie lechem meen ha aretz.* Blessed are You, O Lord our God, King of the Universe, who brings forth bread from the land." I placed matzo in his cupped hands and asked him to release the ushers to serve our church family. There was no response.

I thought perhaps he hadn't heard me, so I repeated myself. Still nothing. He simply stood there, slightly bowed, staring at the bread. So I released the ushers to serve the people.

As time went by, a holy hush seemed to fall on the assembly as if we all sensed something special was happening, but none of us knew exactly what. As more time passed and Pastor Stovall still wasn't responding, I could see the security team getting uneasy, perhaps wondering if something was physically wrong with him. And yet, there remained a quiet peace and calmness in the sanctuary.

After several minutes, I reached for the third cup, the Cup of Redemption. Again, I quoted from Luke 22, "In the same way, after the supper he took the cup saying, 'This cup is the New Covenant in my blood, which is poured out for you.'" I then pronounced the traditional Hebrew blessing, *"Baruch atah Adonai, Eloheinu melech ha olam, porei pre ha gofen.* Blessed are you, O Lord our God, King of the Universe who brings forth the fruit of the vine."

I turned to offer Pastor Stovall the Cup of Redemption. By then he had begun to respond, but hesitantly, as if still in a daze. Again, I released the ushers and called for the worship team to join me on the stage to conclude the service with a song of worship and gratitude to

God for what He had done for us in the body and blood of His Son, Jesus, and went to sit back down.

Many minutes later, Pastor Stovall tried to talk but kept stumbling over his words. He seemed to be trying to describe something that had happened to him during the service, especially when I began speaking the blessing over the matzo in Hebrew. But he was so moved that he could barely get any words out. He called me back to the center of the platform to try to explain it to me. He said something about how he had seen Jesus. I didn't know what to make of it all, and clearly, neither did he. Yet I could sense God had done something very special that night.

As the worship music concluded, Pastor Stovall left the platform. I remained in the auditorium to speak and pray with a few people before going to find him to see how he was doing.

WHAT DOES THIS MEAN?

Back in the green room I saw a man undone. His face was soaked with tears. Pastor Stovall usually had no trouble talking freely, but he was struggling to put words together. The ones that made it out came slowly. He seemed stunned, as if he had just experienced something very much outside the normal church experience.

I offered to leave him alone, but he said he wanted me to stay. He seemed to hope I could give him some kind of context to what he had just seen and heard. It took time for him to find the words, but eventually he told me that when he had taken the matzo bread and I began to speak in Hebrew, my voice had changed into another that seemed to fill the room. (I discovered weeks later that other people had the same experience that night!)

That's when he became aware that Jesus was standing right there on the platform with us.

I summarize what he said here as best I can recall, as he stumbled and paused often:

> I never saw Jesus's face, but I knew it was Him. The sense of love and strength that came from Him was overpowering. I had no sense of guilt or unworthiness, I was family, I belonged there...
>
> I think I was invited to a Passover celebration in Heaven...Is that possible? Does Heaven observe these special feasts with Jesus right there? The apostles were all there, gathered around a white table, and there were beautiful translucent columns and tons of people.
>
> I couldn't see any faces, but I knew I was loved intensely...I had no shame. I belonged there...I was family.

This encounter with Jesus would profoundly affect Pastor Stovall and his wife, Kerri, but we had no idea then how intensely it would affect the life and worship of Celebration Church— and my own house, as well. As a result of it, a lot of things would come front and center: the Lord's table and covenant, the Lord's Prayer, the biblical calendar of feasts and celebrations, and the centrality and importance of our homes, to name a few. We would experience a dynamic activation of the prophetic voice of the Holy Spirit in the preaching, teaching, and worship from that point on. God would use the encounter to begin to equip us as families and smaller groups to gather, commune, and worship Him, preparing us for a time we couldn't even imagine that was just around the next bend in the road.

Very early on I remember Pastor speaking about a time when we wouldn't be allowed to meet—when large gatherings would not be permitted. I always thought he must be speaking about the Great Tribulation during the time of the Antichrist. Little did we know he was really seeing a worldwide event that is now known as the COVID-19 pandemic.

CHAPTER 5

As It Is in Heaven

The days, weeks, and months that followed Pastor Stovall's encounter with Jesus were filled with a lot of questions as we grappled to understand what he saw and heard that night. The most difficult days were the ones immediately following the vision. Trying to tell a nervous flock what had just happened to the shepherd and what it might mean for us all was not easy.

The two days following Good Friday traditionally saw the largest attendance at Celebration because it was Easter weekend. But that year, the two Sunday morning services were anything but traditional as Pastor Stovall sat on the stage with his wife, Kerri, in a question-and-answer session intended to bring some clarity and understanding to the situation. This seemed necessary since Celebration had never experienced anything like this before; visions were not only irregular, but ones such as this were unheard of in this modern megachurch.

He pointed to the biblical accounts of similar "waking visions" in the Scriptures, such as the one Peter experienced in Acts 10.

Pastor Stovall said he would be trying to make sense of it all himself for some time to come. I believe it took tremendous courage on his part to share candidly and lead boldly into whatever God had planned for him and the church without knowing all the details.

Eventually, many changes stemming from that vision would adjust our future plans and functions as a church family, but one was immediate and powerful: Celebration would no longer be a church of systems that was simply building a large organization. We would be a covenant family focused on rearing sons and daughters of God— disciples sold out to knowing and walking with Jesus. Our worship would no longer be limited by the clock; instead, we would be a church that worshiped in spirit and in truth. The prophetic, or *now* voice of God, would be welcome, and the altar (the area immediately in front of the platform) would no longer just be a place for offerings; it would be expanded to minister to whomsoever the Lord would bring—folks who call Celebration home, the stranger, the seeker, the hurting, the addicted.

The weekly staff prayer and teaching times became powerful hours of worship, sharing, and testimonies of how God was working in individual lives throughout all the departments of the church. The teaching from the pulpit became revelatory. Scripture verses that we had read a hundred times suddenly became fresh and alive with inspiration and motivation. The fountains in front of the building were transformed into baptismal tanks that were well used after every service. The service times changed to make room for the extended periods of worship and ministry.

It was obvious to everyone that a major shift had taken place, and the whole church family was on board.

ON EARTH AS IT IS IN HEAVEN

In the weeks that followed, staff meetings turned into prayer meetings as we sought to bring context to what Pastor Stovall had seen and heard during the Passover encounter and how that influenced the church's expression and direction as a body. We all experienced a tremendous sense of anticipation and excitement because the Bible was our textbook, and the Holy Spirit was our teacher. He would be the One to guide us through the hours of prayer and interpretation to make sense of it all.

One shocker that became obvious that night was that there was apparently a Passover event taking place in Heaven while we were celebrating in Jacksonville. Pastor had seen a large white table set with the unleavened bread and the cup of wine, with men sitting around it that he sensed were the disciples of Yeshua. But there was also a huge multitude of other people present. Everyone had a place. They were full of peace and joy. They were loved and they belonged; it was like a huge family celebration. The furniture and columns in the room were made of some kind of translucent blue stone, perhaps alabaster, and other heavenly materials. While Pastor Stovall was not sure about all the details, two things were very clear to him: he was standing with Jesus in Heaven, and they were celebrating the Passover.

Wait a minute. Are we saying Heaven might still be observing or remembering these holy days even after the risen Messiah returned from His mission in Jerusalem? We wrestled with what that could mean for us still here on Earth awaiting His imminent return. The questions seemed to vastly outnumber the answers at first. What would the consequences be for us and the church if we weren't ready for the answers when they came?

I must say that in the weeks following the encounter, my admiration for Pastor Stovall Weems grew by leaps and bounds. I remember him saying many times, "I am not quite sure what this all means, or where this is taking us, but I have to remain faithful to what I have seen and heard." As the whole counsel of the Word of God, the Scriptures became our roadmap for bringing clarity and context to the story unfolding around us. The Gospel of peace and reconciliation with God is built upon the "lively stones" of the apostles and the prophets (1 Peter 1:25). Thus, we continually returned to the wisdom and revelation found in our Bibles for the understanding we so desperately desired.

During the first staff meeting after Easter, as we all prayed and worshiped the Lord, I turned to the Psalms of David. Psalm 25:12–14 seemed to strike a strong nerve of understanding in my heart, so I read the verses aloud:

> Who is the man who fears the Lord?
> Him will he instruct in the way that he should choose.
> His soul shall abide in well-being,
> and his offspring shall inherit the land.
> The friendship of the Lord is for those who fear him,
> and he makes known to them his covenant. (ESV)

"That's it," Pastor Stovall sobbed, "Jesus showed me His covenant." The declaration of these verses brought such a loud verbal response from him that we knew we were traveling in the right direction. Still, many of us wondered where this would lead.

A KAIROS TIME

Peter preached that Jesus "must remain in heaven until the time for the final restoration of all things, as God promised long ago through his holy prophets" (Acts 3:21 NLT). These words used by Peter after the lame beggar was miraculously healed have been critical to discovering *what, why,* and *when.*

Notice, for instance, that he does not use the term *season* instead of *time,* and he does not refer to a *revival* but a *restoration.* The word "time," or *kairos* in the Greek, is specific, whereas "season" is more general. Meanwhile, "revival," in the Western mind, has a certain spontaneous nature to it, like a surprise breakout of Heaven, whereas "restoration" has the sense of a methodical, intentional process over a period of time.

Some fifty years ago, Derek Prince wrote a book titled *The Parallel Restoration of the Church and Israel.* And I must say that the parallel events in the life of Israel and the Church are rather striking:

1. The renewal of faith in the West took place alongside the surge of Zionism at the turn of the twentieth century.
2. The rise of Charismatic and Pentecostal expressions took place during the restoration of the State of Israel in the late 1940s.
3. The Jesus Movement broke out in the mid-1960s as Jerusalem was reunited as the undivided, eternal capital of the State of Israel in 1967.

4. A powerful revival of worship music began about the same time as Israel and was saved from the near disaster of the Yom Kippur War of 1973. Christian music companies that would lead the world in worship like Maranatha! Music, Integrity, and Vineyard all established their roots in that time.

5. As Israel has continued to grow in population, size, and economic influence, we have seen the propagation of teaching, evangelistic, apostolic, and prophetic ministries and the power of the Holy Spirit in the Church worldwide.

Therefore, Friday, March 30, 2018, has come to have the same significance in my mind as some of the events listed above. That night, Heaven intentionally highlighted with bright colors the calendars of the Church and Israel. Jesus made an unprecedented appearance in Jacksonville to announce the *time* had begun to *restore* all things.

I believe we are now beginning to experience the restoration of ourselves as the Ecclesia (Church), as well as an outpouring of love and support for the restoration of Israel and the imminent return of the King.

A Powerful Prayer

During Yeshua's famous Sermon on the Mount, recorded in Matthew 6:9–13, He spent a few powerful moments on the subject of prayer. One section has become especially significant and prophetic during this new time we are now in:

Our Father in heaven,
hallowed be your name.
Your kingdom come,
your will be done,
on earth as it is in heaven. (ESV)

What a thought-provoking expression. How is it possible to operate here on Earth "as it is in Heaven"? Solomon asks the rhetorical
question, "Who has gone up to Heaven and come down?" (Proverbs
30:4 NIV). In the famous discourse with Rabbi Nicodemus, Jesus says,
"No one has ever gone into Heaven except the one who came from
Heaven—the Son of Man" (John 3:13 NIV). The Scriptures simply do
not tell us much about the day-to-day life of Heaven. We get a brief
glimpse of the Garden of Eden in Genesis and receive prophetic
glimpses into Heaven with the prophets and the Revelation of John,
but that's about it.

But we do get a close, personal look at the life of the One who
came from Heaven to show us how to live as sons and daughters of
Yahweh. Jesus says, "I tell you the truth, the Son…can only do what
He sees his Father doing" (John 5:19 NIV). So it only makes sense that
in order to see the Kingdom come on Earth "as it is in Heaven," we
should do what Jesus did. He preached the Kingdom, healed the sick,
and cast out the kingdom of darkness. He was a living Torah who
loved God and His neighbor as Himself. He kept the holy days and
the Sabbath, because He saw His Father do it!

So what are we to make of these holy days, or "Feasts of Israel" as
some call them, that played such a major role in the life and times of
Israel and the first-century believers? They have been ignored,

displaced, or replaced by the Church for the last 1,900 years. Is it because they have been waiting for a particular time to be expressed and re-embraced by the Church in a way that God would use to provoke Israel to jealousy, as Paul argues in the Book of Romans?

Why would Yeshua choose to make such a dramatic appearance in Jacksonville if it were not for the fact that Good Friday was also the first night of Passover? Is it possible He was demonstrating to all of us that Heaven was indeed celebrating the Passover with the Lamb on that very *moed*, or appointed time? If so, then is it time for His body here on Earth to be demonstrating His Kingdom as it is in Heaven? Is it possible that this awakening could be a big part of the "fullness of the Gentiles" that the Apostle Paul says in Romans 11:25 will provoke Israel to jealousy and cause her to seek the God of Abraham?

We wrestled with these questions as a team at Celebration. If Heaven still celebrates the Passover, does that mean all the other feasts are practiced there as well? What about the Feast of Tabernacles that Zechariah says the whole earth will celebrate when the Messiah returns and saves Jerusalem? What about the weekly celebration of rest? After all, doesn't Jesus call Himself the "Lord of the Sabbath"? Historically, New Covenant believers have found little agreement on these issues. But as we prayed, studied, and listened, the answers we received proved to be transformational.

A TIME TO RESTORE

There is a noise, there is a sound;
there is a cry from the depths of our hearts…
Heaven come down.

I co-wrote and recorded those lyrics from "Song of the Beautiful Bride" years ago for Integrity Music. As I mentioned earlier, sounds have the potential to change the atmosphere, our moods and thought processes, and even to invoke the presence of the spirit realm.

My life has been defined by the sounds created over my six decades of life. The journey to discover the sound of the Roar from Zion and the Thunder from Jerusalem that began in the fall of 2017 with the Prophet Joel has now become something of a movement. And the events that have illuminated the pathway to capturing that sound in Jerusalem in 2018 have been both remarkable and amazing.

Christ's disciples asked, "Lord, are you at this time going to restore the kingdom to Israel?" (Acts 1:6 NIV). Those few words have provoked more doctrines, theories, and theologies than one can imagine. What do you think the disciples of Yeshua the Messiah really meant when they asked Him that?

What did the Kingdom look like in their minds? How large was it? What area of land would it occupy? To be a kingdom, there would have to be a king. Would Jesus remain in Jerusalem and live in a palace? Would there be big changes in the Temple? Would the Temple even be needed anymore? What about holy days, celebrations, and all the traditions that have marked Jews as a family and the People of God?

Do we honestly think they were asking Jesus simply to improve or strengthen the condition of the kingdom in Israel—or were they asking Him to be the King of the Jews and rule and reign over the whole earth from Jerusalem? The answer is obvious. In the same way, we are saying today, "Lord, we don't need another revival to improve our condition here. We need *restoration*, to return things to their original intended condition, to restore what has been depleted and lost." In short, we need His Kingdom to come and His will to be done *on Earth as it is in Heaven.*

This bold prayer Jesus taught us to pray goes a lot deeper than many might be willing to consider. To live it and believe it has cost people their jobs, reputations, families, and even their very lives— beginning with those who walked most closely with Jesus Himself. Worshipers through the ages have been tortured, brutalized, perse- cuted, abandoned, disowned, burned at the stake, fed to wild animals in colosseums, sawn in two, and more for wanting to experience life *on Earth as it is in Heaven.* Often it seems like organized religion hates the true Kingdom and resists it because those leaders have no pre- eminence, no position of power or wealth, in the Kingdom of God.

Even here in my own city of Jacksonville, our beautiful palm-lined beaches were once stained with the blood of hundreds of French Huguenots who had fled the religious tyranny of Rome and Paris in the sixteenth century. In 1565, these French Protestant worshipers were slaughtered at the Matanzas Bay with bayonets and swords for daring to imagine a different kingdom on Earth than what they had been forced to embrace.

One thing is clear to us here: We are stewards, not rulers. We are a family, not a corporation. Yes, Jesus has anointed some as pastors, teachers, prophets, evangelists, and even apostles for the building up of His body here and edifying the saints. But the King's subjects are all equal. We are all family. Only the King gets to sit on the throne, for He alone is worthy.

Jesus Himself declared and demonstrated that the leaders He has chosen can easily be identified. They are the ones wearing a towel around their waists, washing the dusty feet of those in need of cleans- ing. They are the ones caring for orphans and widows in their distress, waiting tables and serving folks in need—in other words, "servant leaders." In 1 Corinthians 4:15, the Apostle Paul states that we may have many teachers, but we have very few fathers. In this generation where youth is idolized and envied, the wisdom and function of fathers is passé. A teacher will tell you what to do, but a father will walk with you and show you how to do it. Just as a father serves his children by guiding them, you can serve others by showing them the truth. We must train others to instill habits that will help them grow to be fathers themselves.

Activation of the Covenant and His Kingdom

CHAPTER 6

THE SABBATH

Pastor Stovall reached out to well-known Bible scholars and teachers, people with a lot of letters after their names, as we continued to seek wisdom on what his encounter meant for our church and the Body of Christ. He didn't want it to lead him or his congregation astray, but rather to stay true to sound biblical doctrine.

To my surprise, the first feast to receive attention wasn't the Passover. Rather, it was the first one listed in Leviticus 23—the Sabbath:

> There are six days when you may work, but the seventh day is a day of sabbath rest, a day of sacred assembly. You are not to do any work; wherever you live, it is a sabbath to the Lord. (Leviticus 23:4 NIV)

As a Jewish believer, *Shabbat* has always been special to me. My parents honored it, and my family and I continue the Shabbat practice today. We have always sought to follow a biblical Jewish lifestyle. For us, it was a matter of conscience. We didn't preach the Shabbat as a necessity for salvation and made clear to others it was not a way to earn brownie points with God. He intended them for special purposes—but what were those purposes?

When Leviticus 23 describes the seven feasts, they are commonly designated as "the Feasts of Israel." However, that is not what the Bible calls them. YHVH says, "These are *my* appointed festivals, the appointed festivals of the LORD" (Leviticus 23:2 NIV, emphasis mine). Over and over, He reiterates and establishes *His* dominion over those times and the reasons for them. When He refers to the weekly Sabbath in verse 3, He states that it is a "Sabbath *to* the Lord." Yet later He also states it is a "sabbath of rest *for* you" (Leviticus 23:32 NIV, emphasis mine).

These feasts are *to* the Lord, but they are *for* us. What if our understanding of these holy days has been rooted in a misunderstanding of their importance and purpose, both *to* God and *for* us?

We began to see a broader, more meaningful purpose in the heart of God for these annual celebrations, especially the weekly one He calls the Sabbath. With the encounter on Passover/Good Friday in 2018 came a complete reevaluation of everything we thought we knew about the calendar of the Kingdom. As a result, the essentials of our faith and their influence on our daily lives changed. *We saw that the weekly Sabbath rest is God's plan, His antidote for the systematic destruction of the home.*

If we have no real commitment as a family to gather ourselves together for prayer, fellowship, and communion with the Lord, then our homes simply become houses where we eat, sleep, and wash our dirty clothes. This should not be. If we treat these things lightly, we run the risk of completely missing the treasures of life that God has infused into the family from the beginning. As a result of this understanding, Celebration began to instruct the congregation about how to celebrate the Sabbath biblically in their own homes. Returning it to its rightful place here on Earth soon began to yield abundant blessings from Heaven for our families, some of whose stories I'll share shortly.

The family was initiated by Yahweh to maintain a sense of being a holy nation, a royal priesthood, a people belonging to God. Therefore, these appointments would be *family* gatherings to bring instruction, correction, and training in righteousness for all as they communed together.

But why were these traditions commandments and not suggestions? Simple: Human nature being what it is, we quickly give way to personal preferences or opinions rather than doing what we see our Father do (John 5:19). Comfort and convenience exert a powerful influence on the soul. Unless there are serious consequences for our actions, the carnal man will go his own way faster than we often think possible. For example, how many times have you adjusted your speed because you noticed a police car in your rearview mirror or sitting on the side of the highway? We naturally push the boundaries as humans, which *can* be a great thing. But when the boundaries keep us safe from our own dangerous curiosity, we have to slow down to learn why they are there before we cause an accident. Yahweh gave us His law to prevent these types of spiritual calamities.

When the Lord called Abraham, He did so for a specific purpose. He was looking for a man who would believe Him, someone through whom He could raise a family and restore His plan to bring Heaven to Earth. Isn't this exactly what Jesus taught us to pray in Matthew 6?

If God's plan is to build a loving, faithful family on Earth, what do you suppose the enemy might plan? To do everything in his power to destroy the family, the heavenly reflection of God on Earth, of course. Divide, separate, then conquer.

And isn't that what we see today? The greatest evil we face in Western culture is the destruction of the traditional family unit established by God. From using the television as a babysitter starting in the 1950s to the sexual revolution of the 1960s, the anti-God attitudes of the 1970s, the glorification of Hollywood and liberalism in the 1980s, the invention of the internet in the 1990s and social media in the 2000s, the addictive use of cell phones, the spread of radical feminism and the gay-rights agenda—the list goes on and on. Clearly, the family unit as described in the Bible is relentlessly under attack.

With this understanding, I have begun to see the Sabbath through fresh eyes. *It is God's cultural antidote for the destruction of our families.* Every seven days, no matter how important we might think any task might be, we are told to put it aside for the safety and security of our homes. At sundown on Friday night, all business ceases. We gather the entire family together at the table, where we remember and sanctify the Lord and His presence. There is an order for how we do this because it is helpful for purpose and context. We look one another in the eye and speak blessings and love over each other as we let the rest of the world roll on by. We enjoy a special meal with foods that help us remember and celebrate Jesus, the Lord of the Sabbath. We say "Shabbat shalom" to one another and forget the tyranny of our cell phones. Sabbath night is special, and everyone around our table knows *he or she* is special as well. This is the Sabbath rest of God. We don't allow anything to steal these few precious moments from us.

You can actually feel the rest and pleasure of God as the family settles in for an evening of fellowship and peace—*shalom*.

We are told in Genesis 2 simply that God finished the work He had been doing on the sixth day, so He rested and blessed the seventh day, making it holy. In Leviticus 23 we learn that this Sabbath of rest is unto the Lord. Exodus 20 gives three commandments for us to observe: remember, rest, and keep it holy—distinct and unique. But Isaiah 58:13–14 tells us all the blessings God gives for resting and remembering this special day.

> If you keep your feet from breaking the Sabbath
> And from doing as you please on *my* holy day,
> If you call the Sabbath a delight, and the Lord's holy day
> honorable,
> And if you honor it by not going your own way
> And not doing as you please or speaking idle words,
> Then you will find your joy in the Lord,
> And I will cause you to ride on the heights of the land,
> And to feast on the inheritance of your father Jacob.
> The mouth of the Lord has spoken. (NIV, emphasis added)

According to the Bible, there are really only three commandments for the Sabbath: rest, remember, and keep it holy. Only when the rabbis set forth the traditions of religious life did we begin to find an unbelievably long and complex list of rules to help us understand what "rest and remember" actually mean. (In some homes, even the toilet paper must be portioned prior to the Sabbath so as not to break the rule of "resting" and "doing no regular work.")

The idea of resting and not doing any regular work is fairly easy to understand. But "remembrance" can take on a deeper understanding when we see it in the context of a family celebration. The word "remember" can be defined simply as "to recall," like a mental exercise; however, if we break it down, it gets better. "Re-" is a prefix meaning "again"; "member" could be construed as "a person belonging to a unique group"—as in a family. So perhaps the Sabbath was meant to be a weekly gathering of family members to set aside their work, honor the God who created them, and enjoy the blessings of being a family in the Kingdom. To "remember" was to regather all the family members for this purpose.

Could this have been what Jesus was speaking about at the Last Supper during Passover when He said, "Whenever you do this, do it in remembrance of Me"? In other words, "When you share this covenant meal, don't simply recall who I am, but remember My Body, My family. Bring them all back to the table where we are one, Jew and Gentile, male and female, all races, all generations—and I will meet with you there."

Early in the process to make sense of the encounter, Pastor Stovall wanted my family to demonstrate how we celebrate the Sabbath to the entire church staff. So at the next staff meeting, my son Nathan and his wife, Malki, stood in front of 150 people and shared the design for celebrating Shabbat in their home. It was well received by everyone and brought plenty of questions about the necessity of Hebrew for the blessings, distinguishing between the challah instead of matzo, etc.

After this remarkable time of sharing, I turned my cell phone back on only to be greeted by the most amazing message from Jerusalem. It came from a streaming news source. The timing couldn't have been more astounding. Adam Eliyahu Berkowitz had just posted a statement from Rabbi Yoel Schwartz, head of the Sanhedrin's Noa-hide Court, stating, "One of the reasons the Messiah has yet to reveal himself is because the non-Jewish nations are not keeping the Sabbath." The rabbi also put out a call for the nations (Gentiles) to keep the Sabbath and for the Jews to help them in this mission. You could have knocked me over with a feather. Here we were, doing exactly what the rabbi announced would speed the appearing of the Messiah.

Let's face it. The Church has done a poor job of demonstrating the Messiah to the children of Israel over the past two millennia. In fact, she has done almost the exact opposite as that rabbi showed me so many years ago in that impromptu debate. And now we have religious Jews asking the Church to help them reveal the Messiah?

HOW WE CELEBRATE

Thirty years ago, when my family left Beth Messiah Congregation for Chicago, we had a vision to establish a Messianic fellowship within the context of a local church. We wanted to live out what the Apostle Paul described in Ephesians 2 as the "One New Man." We intended to be an integral part of the life and ministry of the church. On Friday evenings, we would call the city to join us for a Shabbat service of worship and teaching that would give some context for the Jewish community to join with us. We never had the opportunity to fulfill that vision, but the dream remained alive.

Now, many years later, we are in Jacksonville. Shabbat, the Kingdom, and the revealing of the One New Man remain our passion and purpose. Our dream has always been to see the fullness of the Gentiles described in Romans 11 that would provoke Israel to jealousy, and thus spur the return of Jesus our Messiah. And as a result of the encounter with Yeshua that Pastor Stovall had, we are exploring more about how the Sabbath can become a greater part of the rhythms of Christian life and worship.

Surprisingly, the questions have not been so much about *why*, but *how* do we celebrate? The Sabbath celebration and pattern for rest and renewal is thousands of years old, going as far back as creation. Our Heavenly Father was the first to honor the seventh day. As we saw earlier, He declared it to be holy, and He blessed it (Genesis 2:2–3). The Sabbath is the only day that received a name; all the others are numbered. The Sabbath was instituted before the Law of Moses, which was given about 3,500 years ago—so it is literally about as ancient as it can get.

We begin after sundown on Friday evening. We gather our family around the dinner table, because a biblical day begins *after* sundown. It *begins* with rest. My wife sets the table with special plates. She has prepared a special meal. My great-grandmother's Shabbat candle-sticks, which have been passed on to my wife, have a prominent place on the table.

When everyone is gathered, my wife lights the Sabbath candles and speaks a blessing that recognizes God as the Ruler of the Universe, Yeshua as the Messiah and the Light of the World, and us as being sent by Him as lights into the world. With that, we sanctify the time and space as holy and invite His manifest presence as the Lord of the Sabbath and of our home.

Next, as the father of the house, I take the special bread—the challah that is braided with three strands and made especially for this day—lift it up, and give thanks to God for His provision. In believers' homes, it is broken and received as the Body of the Messiah, remembering the covenant He made with us. Next, we take the cup of wine, lift it up with prayers of thanksgiving, and receive it as the blood of the covenant in Yeshua. Then prayers are prayed for my wife and our children. We all sit together and enjoy a special meal without television or cell phones. We talk about our day, family business, or whatever else brings peace and connection. This is not a "date night"; we simply stay home and enjoy our family. If we have invited guests, we spend time with them and include them in the prayers and everything else.

SABBATH BLESSINGS

The effects of the Sabbath are more than emotional relaxation, although it is certainly relaxing. I have witnessed the healing and rejuvenation the Shabbat brings on many occasions. One instance that really stands out in my memory involves one of our own Celebration family members—Pastor Wayne Lanier and his wife, Diana, who have been on staff for many years.

In the late spring of 2010, Diana was diagnosed with an extremely aggressive form of breast cancer. She was simultaneously diagnosed with diabetes and high blood pressure, which the cancer treatments exacerbated. Many excruciating procedures proved to be only the beginning of a long and painful three-year journey. The side effects of rigorous chemo and radiation left Diana with severe damage to the nerves in her feet, lower legs, and hands. The combination of relentless pain and numbness in her feet required constant vigilance to avoid accidental injury. These symptoms progressed to the point where Diana couldn't stand or walk for significant periods of time. She could only leave the house for brief outings, using an electric cart for mobility, and she'd have to spend days regaining her energy before she could consider going out again.

As a pastor's wife and homeschool mother of six children, Diana could barely function. The whole family spent many days simply praying for her healing. Daily the family would speak scriptures over her and anoint her body with oil. They continued to do this for nine years as her condition worsened.

But that all changed when they remembered the Sabbath as a family once again.

As 2018 drew to a close, Diana and Wayne had an encounter with the Holy Spirit during a Wednesday night service. The Lord acknowledged all they had done to pray, speak the Word, and trust Him for healing, but He challenged Wayne with these words: "You have done well in all these things, but you have spent all your energy focused on the problem and trying to fix the symptoms. If you will put Me back in the center of your family, I know exactly what's needed."

They were also reminded of the priestly blessing in Numbers 6:23–27: "When you speak this, you are putting My name on your family," the Holy Spirit said to Wayne. "When you put My name on them, I Myself will bless them, and My blessing knows exactly what is needed in every person and in every situation. Let Me be on the front lines on your behalf."

So, the next Friday evening, Wayne and Diana celebrated Shabbat with prayer and communion as a family. Two days later, after church, Diana felt surprisingly well-rested. She said she might be up for a walk on the beach. She ended up walking for hours without needing to sit down and rest. The whole family was full of both worry and wonder. Diana was filled with questions. *Did this really just happen? Am I really feeling this good?* Wayne led them in prayers of thanks on the way home, and later that night, Diana told him, "It feels like the Lord is healing me."

The next morning, Diana checked her blood sugar as usual. What she saw was shocking. She called out to Wayne to come see. Her blood sugar was within the normal range for the first time in years, and it has remained there every day since.

That next weekend, Diana shared with me that she was getting ready for church when she felt a strange sensation...*the floor*. As the tears ran down her face, all she could say was, "Jesus, I love You so much. Thank You, thank You, thank You."

Every Friday night the family gathered around the table to celebrate Shabbat. Every week Diana got better and better. In January 2019, Diana and Wayne went to the altar with the youth at a conference, and they danced and worshiped the Lord with all their hearts. That was when Diana realized, "I'm totally healed!"

Even today, though the family can't all meet in person, they still take the day to recognize the Sabbath over video chat to share in the fellowship and rejuvenation of the rest the King has provided.

PREPARATION FOR A PANDEMIC

The Sabbath would prove particularly powerful during the COVID-19 pandemic of 2020. In late February, a small team from Celebration Church led about seventy pastors and their wives from fourteen nations in remembering the Feast of Esther (*Purim* in Hebrew) at the Auschwitz death camp in Poland. We walked the grounds and finished the day by sharing communion in front of one of the vile cattle cars that had transported so many Jewish souls into one of the worst nightmares ever perpetrated upon mankind. We prayed for Israel, the Jewish community of the world, and repented on behalf of a Church that has been mostly silent about all those things over the last seven decades.

The next day we planned to board an El Al jetliner to Tel Aviv for an international conference in Jerusalem. Afterward, we arranged to fly across the Atlantic to Guatemala, where I was to lead worship for another conference that was to include the newly elected president.

But that morning we awoke to some startling news: the world was beginning a lockdown process that would suspend all travel and business internationally and within the United States for months on end. When we finally arrived back home, we realized we had barely escaped being forced to quarantine for weeks in New York City.

Fortunately, nearly two years earlier Pastor Stovall had begun asking, "What would we do if for some unforeseen reason we are not allowed to meet together as a church?" I must admit that during those two years leading up to the shutdown of March 2020, that question would always conjure up some scene from the Book of Revelation when the Antichrist would rule the world.

But when COVID hit, I saw the genius plan of God in the Shabbat. We were already being trained and prepared to *be* the Church in our homes. We didn't need a huge building with expensive equipment, programs for all ages and interests, multimillion-dollar budgets, etc. We were all priests of a new covenant designed to transform the world one person at a time, one family at a time, one neighborhood at a time. The Shabbat that our Father modeled for us in Genesis 1 was the blueprint—not for some mandatory religious exercise, but for a pattern and a rhythm of life that would help us model a Kingdom "on Earth as it is in Heaven."

At that point, the other feasts of the Lord began to take on deeper and more profound meaning as well. Instead of being filed into the good old *fulfilled* category along with the rest of the Old Testament, perhaps there were some things we had been missing there.

Those feasts were also good for hearing from each other, mending broken or strained relationships, and being a large family with a common call and destiny. We might liken them to a State of the Union Address. But in Israel's case, observing these appointed times, like the Sabbath, was not left up to the people; God knows what happens when He does that. Before long we would lose track of His sacraments, just like a New Year's resolution, gym membership, or diet program.

The Sabbath is not complicated. Quite the opposite—it was set in place by God to force us to simplify and rest. In today's rushed Western culture, it is decidedly countercultural. Thanks to God's once again roaring from Zion, we are seeing this appointed time reinstated in the Church today—not only in Jacksonville, but beyond as well. It is not the only special biblical event being restored on Earth as it is in Heaven, but it is perhaps one of the most foundational.

CHAPTER 7

THE HEALING
OF THE TABLE

W ithout a doubt, the greatest revelation that came to us during
this encounter of the Kingdom has concerned the power of
the table. I suppose that should not be surprising, since what Pastor
Stovall observed was the celebration of the Passover meal around the
table in Heaven.

But "the table" is broader than the Passover. It is where the covenant of family, rest, and salvation are highlighted and celebrated.
Growing up in a Messianic Jewish home brings certain traditions and
practices that most Christian families do not enjoy, especially when
it comes to Shabbat and the other Feasts of the Lord.

Before Passover 2018, we viewed these celebrations and traditions
as family affairs that were kept pretty much to ourselves. But with
the news that Heaven also celebrates these special times, our church
family now sees them as great opportunities to share the joy with
neighbors and family beyond those living in the same house.

For instance, one tradition for the Sabbath is to bake (or purchase) special Shabbat bread, called challah. The delicious recipe sometimes contains raisins, cinnamon, or both and is coated with a lovely honey glaze. It is often made of three strands of dough braided together before baking. The strands resemble arms folded across the chest in a position of rest, reminding us that Shabbat is a time of rest and restoration.

My daughter-in-law Malki has become quite the expert at the art of making challah, so her Sabbath breads are highly sought after these days. But instead of keeping them for her own family, she often makes many more loaves to give to friends and neighbors to enjoy. Every Friday afternoon, the home she and my son Nathan share is surrounded by cars and golf carts piloted by eager Jewish and Christian believers looking for bread.

Another benefit of enjoying and celebrating the Sabbath table is that it brings great confidence and a context for sharing the Good News of Jesus. For example, Nathan and Malki recently asked a Jewish neighbor to join them for a Shabbat dinner. As a result, the man asked if I could join them another time and we could all show him the Messiah in the Hebrew Scriptures.

Another Jewish neighbor has had a change of heart regarding Jesus after enjoying a Sabbath meal at Nathan and Malki's table, and his ten-year-old son has been asking to go to church. These interactions are not isolated cases; they're happening all over the place now as a result of the resurgence of celebrating Jesus, the Lord of the Sabbath, around the table.

When I was growing up, I saw Christian families with traditions of going to church on Sunday morning and then enjoying a big family meal together after the service. In fact, many a Sunday morning sermon was laced with humor about the message being shortened so as not to ruin the Sunday roast cooking at home. I also remember a time when almost every shop or store was closed early on Saturday afternoon and all day Sunday. However, I would bet that most people under the age of forty can't remember a Sunday when anything was closed (except for Chick-fil-A, of course).

So it was with great curiosity and a bit of trepidation that our Gentile church of twelve thousand in Jacksonville decided to give this weekly feast of rest and family its proper place again. We saw miracles of physical healings, restoration of family relationships, children repenting to their parents for being rude or disrespectful, and on and on—so much so that we had to hold entire services for people to testify of God's goodness and faithfulness. The Shabbat table has now become such a place of covenant and restoration that many people in the church are opening their homes for neighbors and even total strangers to enjoy.

For example, my son and his wife were out with a group of friends for dinner on a Friday night at a Cracker Barrel restaurant. As the sun was setting, one of them took out a couple of votive candles and placed them on the table. Then they asked the waitress for some crackers and a glass of grape juice to share. Right there at the Cracker Barrel, they lit the Sabbath lights, invited the presence of God, shared communion, and prayed for each other. The hostess saw what was happening and asked if she could join them—and a waitress began crying!

Such an impactful moment reminds me of the experience I had on an overseas flight when I saw a documentary on the making of *Fiddler on the Roof*. Most of the actors and actresses were Jews, as were the director and crew, but they had no real religious background. It was great fun for them pretending to be poor *shtetl* Jews of eastern Europe and Russia with the clothing, the sets, and the dancing.

But something strange happened during the filming of the Sabbath meal and prayers. As the actors sat around an old wooden table on rickety chairs and lit the Sabbath candles with the songs of blessing and *Shabbat shalom*, nearly every eye filled with tears. Lips began to tremble as they all wondered what they were actually experiencing during a staged performance. One of them asked, "What's happening here?" Another said, "I had no idea what I was missing." It was tender, moving, deeply emotional, even transformational.

As a direct result of open doors and open hearts around the table, our church families are now experiencing the joy of giving in other ways as well. Some of our neighbors have started a community Bible study in their home every other week. Many from the church want to learn Hebrew so they can study the Bible in the original language.

I've experienced this same unifying effect in my own life. A family moved in down the street a little while back, and I told my wife that we needed to meet them—but we didn't do it right away. As time went on, I became embarrassed that we had never greeted them. Then one Sunday, when we were coming home from a service around two in the afternoon, I saw my neighbor standing at his mailbox. "That's it!" I told my wife. "I want to grab some of my music CDs or something and go say, 'Hello.'"

But before I could do anything, the man ran over from across the street. He's an athletic guy with a shaved head, so he can seem a bit imposing if he's running toward you. I didn't know what to think, but before I could get out of the car, he reached in and hugged me. Then, because the door was open and my wife was on the other side, he reached over and hugged her too! I was stunned when he said, "I've been watching you on your broadcast. The table celebrations have brought such life into my home. Please come and have dinner with us and do communion."

Simply amazing. Here was a complete stranger who lived just a few doors away, inviting us to share the table with him.

UNITY

I was sitting by myself one day a few weeks before Passover 2020, asking the Lord to show us how we might make it special for our church and our city. The thought of a city-wide sit-down seder meal came to mind, but with the COVID-19 shutdown well under way, I knew that would be impossible.

Then it hit me: Why not call my friend Asher Intrater in Jerusalem and ask him to do a live Zoom seder from Israel that our entire community could enjoy? Initially, he didn't think he could do it; Passover in Israel is a huge family celebration and a very busy time for the congregations. But then, Israeli officials announced that because of COVID, no one would be allowed even to cross the street to celebrate the feast that year—in the entire nation!

My next conversation with Asher was quite different, as lockdowns spread all across the world. He was much more excited about my idea. The next thing I knew, he had secured other families around Israel who would lead a portion of the seder meal from their home tables. David Damian, an Egyptian-Arab pastor with a deep love for his Jewish brothers and sisters, would cohost the event and make it a night to remember for followers of Jesus worldwide.

An Egyptian-Arab Christian and an Israeli Messianic Jew would lead the world in prayer and worship to remember the Passover Lamb of God who took away the sins of the world?!? *Was I dreaming?*

As word got out, we began to see that this New Covenant seder would be much more significant than we first imagined—but we still had no idea of the ripple effect it would have across the globe.

The days preceding Passover would be spent in prayer and planning for how to divide the seder meal and which media platforms we would use to unite the Church worldwide. As it turned out, my family was honored to be invited to open and close the celebration from our home in Jacksonville. We enlisted the best video technician from our church to set up the lighting, attach microphones, and test the system. Pastor Stovall and his wife, Kerri, would join us, and my son Joel and his family would fly in from Los Angeles. I knew this would be a Passover to remember, but once again, I had no clue how deeply it would impact my family—or the world.

When the time arrived, we would be joined by more than 140 nations. We would have simultaneous translation in twenty-seven languages. We would take communion with more than one million believers in Jesus by the end of our three-hour Passover celebration. There would be prayer, worship, demonstration, and explanation of that "Last Supper" Jesus celebrated with His disciples two thousand years ago. There would be laughter and joy, sorrow and tears, prayer and praise arising like waves of the sea as we sat around a global table of covenant in thanksgiving to the God who redeemed us all through the blood of His Son, the Lamb of God.

Let me tell you, it was the quickest and most powerful three hours I ever spent gazing into a computer. Before I knew it, it was time for my family to close with the Aaronic blessing of Numbers 6. The weight of what I was asked to do became overwhelming as I wept through each and every word in English and then in Hebrew:

> May the Lord bless you and keep you;
> May the Lord make His face to shine upon you,
> and be gracious unto you.
> And may the Lord lift up His countenance upon you,
> And give you His Shalom.

A holy hush settled over everyone from those 140 nations for several moments before the final "Amen."

Still, we didn't understand the impact of what we had just experienced. Finally, we all agreed that we had to do that again. Pentecost, the Feast of Weeks, was only fifty days away. We agreed to meet again for that sacred time.

THE FAMILY THAT PRAYS TOGETHER

By then our new relationships had begun to grow into full-blown Godly love affairs with each other. Arabs spoke and sang Hebrew. Jews spoke and sang in Arabic. Wisdom, worship, revelation, and love flowed through the computer terminals. We came to realize this was the real reason the internet must have been created in the first place. We were joined by pastors and ministers who are known worldwide but who had never worshiped together. Some men who had openly criticized or opposed each other in the past looked each other in the eyes and repented as the entire world looked on. Arabs and Jews confessed their bitterness and even hatred for one another while Chinese Christians prayed for us all.

On Pentecost, we discovered more than six hundred thousand connections were happening via the internet around the globe. Some families and entire congregations joined by satellite. We still don't know exactly how many people met to worship and pray across the world, but it was all a miracle. We knew Heaven had made an appointment with us for the express purpose of uniting the Body of the Messiah to hear from the King.

It's been said that the family that prays together stays together. As antiquated as that may sound, many studies prove it to be true.

What is the one quality of Jewish life that you would say is most universally admired? Without a doubt, it would have to be family. Does that happen by accident, or could the Jewish lifestyle be inherently designed to promote and protect the family and home? Why is it that in Jewish neighborhoods we see so many shop signs that say, "Horowitz and Son" or "Goldman and Goldman"? I believe you can trace that remarkable bond of love and covenant to the families' dedication to Shabbat meals and worship.

On our Zoom call, we all realized that at this table of covenant in the blood of Jesus, *no one* has reason to boast or to be ashamed. We were truly one body, one holy nation, one people of God, one family from every tribe and tongue. As the Pentecost feast came to a close, I had the opportunity to remind us all of the precious words God spoke in Hebrews 2:11 (NIV):

> Both the one who makes men holy [Jesus],
> And those who are made holy [all of us!] are of the same
> family.
> So Jesus is not ashamed to call them
> Brothers and sisters.

CHAPTER 8

A Double-Edged Sword

I srael and the Ecclesia (the Church) are neither opponents nor
adversaries in God's Kingdom story. They are partners in the salvation of the world. They are in league together, preparing the way for
Yeshua so He may take up His throne in Jerusalem.

Perhaps a hundred years ago that statement might have seemed
preposterous. Yet today, in light of the Roar we are hearing and all
the prophecies that are being fulfilled, it is beginning to make much
more sense.

Our King never intended to do all the work of building His Kingdom. Rather, He has always had a priesthood in the earth that He
enlists to partner in His plans. When YHVH created humanity in
Genesis 1:28, He gave us authority to rule over the planet. He told us
to "fill the earth and subdue it. Rule over the fish of the sea, the birds
of the air, and over every living creature that moves on the ground"
(NIV). Jesus said, "All authority in heaven and earth has been given
to me" (Matthew 28:18 NIV). Not even Jesus could take or assume

authority. It had to be given to Him by His Father, YHVH, the One who has *all* authority.

Furthermore, any authority that is not given by Him—that is usurped or taken by force or deceit—is unlawful. It cannot stand. Jesus also taught us that in order to enter the Kingdom, one must use the front door—namely Him. He is the Door. Anyone who tries to climb over the back wall or dig under the fence is a thief and a robber without authority, for no lawbreaker has authority anywhere.

Our King has given both the Church and Israel authority to act on His behalf to usher in His reign. The restoration of the Church and the restoration of Israel are inherently connected and interdependent. We truly are "brothers from other mothers." We have many *mothers*—tribes and tongues—but only one Father. We were separated soon after rebirth, but I believe it is the will and passion of our Father that we would be reunited at His covenant table. And the fullness of time for that restoration is at hand.

I see this parallel restoration as a great sword in the hands of a mighty warrior. Imagine a huge broadsword. It takes two hands to wield the massive hilt. Above the hilt, a large piece of steel called a cross guard is welded to hold the blade. The blade has two sharp, distinct edges and a massive amount of steel between them, called a "fuller." This fuller has a large, grooved area down the middle, forming a significant gulf between the two edges. These two very sharp edges move along a parallel course that never seems to bring them closer together—until the end. Right at the tip, these two parallel partners sharply change course to meet one another in the middle and form the point of the sword.

This sharp point is where Israel and the Church find themselves coming together in what I would call "The Day of the Lord." Both have their origin in the hand of the Lord; they were separated at the cross guard, and each has traveled along its own course since then. However, they have supported one another in battle. At the journey's end, they swiftly come together to form a sharp point when Israel declares, "*Baruch haba b'shem Adonai*. Blessed is He who comes in the name of the Lord." At that point, the complete Bride is prepared for the Bridegroom.

Yeshua spoke about many events that would take place before the coming of the Lord. There would be wars and rumors of wars, famines, false messiahs, the Gospel would be preached in all the nations, a betrothed Bride would be prepared for her Bridegroom, and Jerusalem would welcome Him to return. The Prophet Daniel saw kingdoms rising and falling in the vision of the statue of gold, silver, bronze, and clay. John the Beloved saw bowls, angels, judgments, and the Great Tribulation before the coming of the Lion of Judah.

Jesus Himself said many difficult things. He said often that He had not come to bring peace, but a sword. Jesus did not come to establish a new religion. Let that sink in: *Jesus was not a Christian*. However, He did preach the Kingdom whenever and wherever He went. What made Him so different from all those who had come before Him was that He not only *declared* the Kingdom, but also *demonstrated* the Kingdom. He told the doubting religious leaders that if they didn't believe His words, they should believe in Him for what He did. It was as if He were saying, "This is what my Father meant when He said to Moses, 'Now if you obey me fully and keep my covenant, then out of all nations you will be my treasured possession. Although the whole earth is mine, you will be for me a kingdom of priests and a Holy nation'" (Exodus 19:5–6 NIV).

THE WORDS WE USE

During this era of reunification, language must be reevaluated. Terminology used casually or without intention can quickly lose its impact and purpose. Words like *time, revival, restoration, kingdom, prophetic*—these all carry a powerful sense of purpose and direction with them unless they are overused or used without clear understanding. In light of what God is doing to reunite His people, I see a need to reassess our vocabulary and clarify terms.

For example, almost the entire thirteenth chapter of the Gospel of Matthew is dedicated to the subject of the Kingdom. In verse 11, Jesus says to His disciples, "The knowledge of the secrets of the kingdom of Heaven has been given to you, but not to them." It seems not everyone who hears or reads about the Kingdom will understand the Kingdom. Yet Jesus taught us to pray, "Let Your kingdom come on earth as it is in Heaven." Using the same words does not mean we share the same understanding.

Believe me, I understand that here in our independent-minded Western culture, words like *obey* and *keep* have been out of style for quite some time. But I would suggest that we have not understood *kingdom* or *covenant* for that very reason. We and our families suffer because we lack even a basic understanding of these terms.

Could this be the reason the Body of Christ is splintered into more than thirty-five thousand denominations today? Our pride produces the blindness that drives a wedge between us and our brothers and sisters in Christ. Is it any wonder we do this when our sinful nature is so self-focused? I have no doubt the enemy takes great pleasure in our turning on one another; but the joke is soon to be on him as we grow closer together and stronger than ever before. As we unite the Father's Kingdom, we mustn't lose focus on our work and our goal.

We must continually remind ourselves of one essential thing as we seek first the Kingdom and His righteousness: Yeshua is the King of the Kingdom. He is the Word made flesh, the Son of God, the Messiah, the Lamb who takes away the sins of the world, the Lion of the Tribe of Judah. As we engage these different aspects of Kingdom life with fresh ears and eyes during this time of restoration, we must remember that we are not worshiping the feasts or the Sabbath. We worship Yeshua, Lord of the Sabbath. Indeed, nothing makes any sense for us outside of Jesus. He is the fullness of the Torah, the fullness of the Godhead in bodily form, and the fullness of the covenant. Any revelation, vision, dream, or visitation that says otherwise did not originate from God.

I say this all because as soon as anyone dares to think outside their denominational box, the heresy police start to track you down. *Judaizer, false prophet*, and *heretic* are all terms I have heard, as well as "You want to put us back under the Law!" It seems that just when I think I've heard it all, another one comes along.

Remember that we are speaking about the restoration of the Church and Israel. Both are going places, seeing and hearing things we haven't seen or heard for quite some time. Don't forget that there was a time when the only believers in Jesus were Jews who loved and served the God of Abraham, Isaac, and Jacob. Wasn't it also true that there was a time when a Gentile couldn't follow the Jewish Messiah unless he became a Jew? (See Acts 15.)

The traditional long sword does not favor one side or the other; it is equal in length, size, and strength until it is finally united at the tip—the sharpest, most effective point. We do not seek a Kingdom that is predominantly Jewish or Ecclesiastic; we seek first His Kingdom and His righteousness. We have crossed into a time when the twin blades of the sword have changed their degrees and have begun to reunite with one another. Like the Passover challah, soon Israel and the Church will be utterly intertwined and connected in our every waking movement—dual strands coming together to form one loaf, one Kingdom. The time is drawing near when we shall worship together as one people.

What we are after now is worship in spirit and in truth. Until the time of the encounter with Pastor Stovall and Yeshua, there may have been a pattern for worship services that paid homage to the timely plan as opposed to the quality of His presence. In our modern contemporary churches, there exists a well-known formula for growth and attendance: "The service should not exceed seventy-five minutes from start to finish." "It should keep a good pace, recognizing the limited attention span of the average Millennial." "Sound levels should be at so many decibels." "Limit the song service to three upbeat songs." "Pay attention to the age of those you permit to be on stage." "Don't allow children in the adult service." There are often more restrictions, but you get the idea.

Pastor Stovall and the team at Celebration have been clear about how the encounter has led them to make significant changes in how they approach church and the worship service. And in this unique time, we all need to do the same—daring to evaluate everything we do by the Scriptures, understanding the times.

Since the day Jesus came to church in Jacksonville, the gloves have come off regarding worship. The flashing digital lights and strict time limitations have given way to an invitation for Heaven to abide with us as we raise a Holy Hallelujah. Worship and praise and their places in the life of a believer are not only taught, but demonstrated in the lives of the worship team and the pastors in the front row. Gone are the days when the pastor stayed behind in the green room while the music team performed for fifteen minutes, leading into the announcement video preparing for the entrance of the teacher. Now the pastor is actively engaged in the worship, listening for the voice of the Holy Spirit to insert a word of encouragement or lead into some ministry time as He directs.

The prophetic voice is more welcome now. Rather than being a spiritual distraction, the Living Word is seen as the grace of God's presence in our midst. The altars are always open for people to come to respond to the voice of God. Attentive staff members are prepared to pray with those who answer the ministry call, and the voice of the Holy Spirit is our daily bread.

SINGING WHAT WE BELIEVE

Since faith comes by hearing, and hearing by the Word of the Lord, it could easily be reasoned that faith comes by singing—singing the Word of God. As humans, we don't usually say what we don't believe. Even the worst of liars struggles to deceive explicitly, often finding ways to dance around the truth. Likewise, to be candid, I often find myself dropping out during portions of modern worship choruses that simply are not true statements of my heart.

Words are important. They can be filled with many different spiritual powers. Words can be sent forth with faith, anointing, power, hope, love, joy, peace, patience, kindness, goodness, long-suffering, and self-control. They can also be empowered by strife, anger, bitterness, rage, slander, pride, malice, greed, and every form of evil. The good or harm they do is real and often quickly felt or recognized. Words can heal and unite, or they can uproot and destroy. We get to choose.

As I mentioned earlier, one of the great watchwords of this fresh Kingdom awakening comes from Matthew 6:10: "May Your kingdom come, and Your will be done on Earth as it is in Heaven." This truth is why I am so committed to singing the Scriptures. I am convicted to sing what God says so I can align my words and my thoughts with His. I want to declare His will into the atmosphere and into the ears of those who hear it…on Earth as it is in Heaven.

I am not alone. Not long ago I was asked to minister the praise and worship at a Messianic rabbis' conference in Orlando, Florida. The guest speaker that day happened to be an associate pastor of a huge evangelical church in Ohio. After finishing my time of worship, I sat down in the darkened auditorium, and then the speaker took the microphone and called my name. "Paul, thank you for not leading us in some 'Jesus is my boyfriend' songs," he said. I was glad the music had given him a voice to truly praise and worship the Lord, but after some time to think about his comment, I became more concerned about what the Body of Christ calls worship music.

It's All about the Pronouns

It really begins with a perspective shift. When you see what God is doing, it changes your perspective. Instead of saying *I*, *me*, or *mine*, you begin saying *ours* and think *family* and *His*.

As strange as it may be to hear in this politically correct culture of ours, pronouns matter. You may have seen that in 2021, when Congress passed a new rule that restricts federal legislators from using terms like *father*, *mother*, *brother*, *sister*, *male*, and *female* during official proceedings. Why is this so offensive to our modern society? Pronouns differentiate between male and female, individuals and groups. When we abuse or misuse pronouns, we become disoriented and can lose focus on the truth, where we belong, and *whose* we are.

In our modern "praise and worship" music, I hear lots of lyrics about personal struggles and conditions of life and very little of the Scriptures. I see far too often that we have been singing *about* God instead of singing *to* Him. Imagine if you were invited to an audience with a king and you walked into his presence and ignored him, simply talking to the person next to you, saying, "Boy, isn't he amazing! What an awesome throne he has. He's really a great ruler. You know, this king has been so good to me." What do you suppose would happen? Besides totally embarrassing yourself—and the king—you might be fortunate to leave that audience with your head still securely on your shoulders.

The Psalmist calls us to "enter His gates with thanksgiving and His courts with praise; give thanks to Him and praise His name" (Psalm 100:4 NIV). Right from the beginning, we see "thanksgiving." Who are we thanking? What are we saying? The Hebrew word used for "thanksgiving" is *todah*, which simply means "thank you." When you receive a gift, you look at the giver and say, "Thank you." And the word used for "praise" here is the Hebrew word *t'hilah*, or "a song of thanksgiving and praise." It is derived from another word, *halal*, from which we get the word *hallelujah* (or *halal Yahweh*). So we could translate this well-known verse this way: "Enter His gates with 'thank you' on your lips and enter His courts with a song of thanksgiving and praise in your mouth." King David tells us that as soon as we enter His gates, we're already speaking to someone else—Him!

There are many Hebrew words for *praise* that give very specific instructions about how to approach a throne. I use them if I'm speaking to worship leaders or songwriters to discover what our purpose is for any song we compose or perform. Are we gathering together to speak to and sing to one another? There's a time for that, obviously, but if we're coming to a sanctuary to worship, that means we have a specific purpose.

The Greek word for worship, *proskuneo*, means: "to kiss towards; to shoot towards like an arrow." When we worship, our praise is shooting toward a specific target. The Hebrew word for worship is *shachah*, and it means "to bow low." When we are bowing low, we are not distracted by what's around us. We're completely focused in a place of humility, submission, and vulnerability. The object of our worship is in front of us. It's not beside us; it's not behind us. We're not thinking about anything else except that which we are totally surrendered to. Shouldn't our language promote that kind of posture?

Passionate praise provokes His presence. We see so often in the Scriptures that God basically ignored the Israelites' prayers when they weren't worshiping Him. He ignored their petitions until they became really serious and cried out to Him—often only after they faced an invading army. When they truly repented and cried out to Him, He sent a deliverer, a judge, a king, a priest, and then ultimately, His Son.

Unfortunately, a lot of our modern choruses do not even use God's name, but simply refer to Him as *He* or *God*. The King of the Universe actually has a name that distinguishes Him from all the other gods. His name is Yahweh, Jehovah, Yeshua, Jesus, El Shaddai, El Elyon, Adonai, Elohim, and many more.

THE NAME OF JESUS

This emphasis on words leads to an important one that has divided the Jewish and Christian believers. To understand the issue, it is critical that we first understand what the Apostle Paul conveyed in Romans:

> I am talking to you Gentiles. Inasmuch as I am the apostle to the Gentiles...I do not want you to be ignorant of this mystery, brothers, so that you may not be conceited: Israel has experienced a blindness in part. (Romans 11:13, 25 NIV)

Paul's warning to the Church at Rome around AD 57 could easily be sent throughout the Ecclesia as a fresh revelation this very day. The Church at Rome was already resisting their Jewish brethren at that point and excluding them from the assembly. Paul reminds them of the condition of Israel in that day. He tells them that Israel has experienced a "blindness" in part, but this hardening is for the benefit of the Gentiles. There is, therefore, no grounds for conceit, a byproduct of pride. It always deceives and inevitably produces blindness in the heart and mind of the one who gives it a place to fester.

It is interesting as well to note that in 1 Corinthians 5, Paul likens the leaven of Passover to pride. Like the bread of affliction, it should be cleansed out of every heart and home before it produces the sin of pride and blindness. So the Church must guard against conceit when seeking to understand their Jewish brothers and sisters, especially when it comes to the use of this most important word.

For nearly two millennia, all of Israel, and Orthodox and religious Jews in particular, have mispronounced (intentionally or ignorantly) the Hebrew name of Jesus. Some won't pronounce His English name at all. The very religious will even spit on the ground when hearing the Name. It is painful to see and hear, but remember that many so-called Christians through the centuries have given Jesus an extremely poor reputation among the Jewish community through their words and deeds. The name of Jesus in Hebrew is *Yeshua*, which is short for *Y'hoshua* or *Joshua*. It means "YHVH saves" or "He will save," as the angel Gabriel said to Miriam (Mary) in Luke 1:31. His Hebrew name is spelled with four letters, *Yod-Shin-Vav-Ayin*, and is pronounced *Ye-SHOO-ah*, with the accent on the second syllable.

Much of the Jewish community shortens His Hebrew name by one letter and calls Him *Yeshu*, which means "may his name and memory be erased forever." Only one small Hebrew letter differentiates between "Salvation" and "may his name be erased." It is the letter *ayin*—which in the pictographic Hebrew alphabet is the image of an eye, the letter that brings sight to the blind.

All of that was in my mind in 2018. What if during the seventieth anniversary of Israel's rebirth, during the seventh decade on the Hebrew calendar, the God of Israel would begin to remove her "blindness in part"? What if He began to open her eyes so she could *see* the missing letter of sight, the *ayin* missing from the Name? What if Israel's eyes could be opened once more to the Name of Yeshua—her salvation and her Messiah?

In fact, what if she is already rapidly regaining her sight? Just as Jesus gave the blind man in Bethsaida eyes to see, Israel has only to have the mud washed from her eyes to acknowledge the glory of her own Messiah.

Awakening to *Yeshua*

I was invited to fly to Jerusalem for a one-night concert in 2018 at the King David Hotel. I normally wouldn't travel such a distance for only one night, but this was Jerusalem, and I knew the host well—

a Nigerian entrepreneur who has hosted me for several one-night events all over the globe, including Rio de Janeiro and Carnegie Hall. And I wasn't going to say no to the opportunity to visit Jerusalem.

When I arrived at Ben Gurion Airport in Tel Aviv early that morning, a driver was waiting for me as usual. We loaded my guitar, suitcase, and equipment into the taxicab and set off to Jerusalem and the King David Hotel—which is not only a historical landmark, but also a luxurious place to stay in the heart of downtown Jerusalem. When we pulled into the tree-lined driveway, my driver pulled right up to the front door, where two smartly uniformed doormen waited at attention. The young man closest to the car opened my door and stood looking at me a moment before sheepishly asking, "Are you the singer?"

I must admit that I was taken by surprise. Here was a Millennial Jewish man who seemed to know me! I answered him with something like, "I might be?"

He leaned into the car before I could get my feet on the pavement and whispered, "I love your *gospel* music." Then he looked over at his friend attending the other front door and said, "He does too." He then took my bags to the front desk, waited while I checked in, and carried my bags and guitar to my room. He followed me in and showed me a few minutes' worth of a video of his senior piano recital at the music academy on his iPhone, then said if I needed any help that night for the concert that he would be pleased to offer his skills at no charge. He gave me his contact information and returned to his post in front of the hotel.

For a few moments I thought perhaps I had just met Rod Serling and was experiencing an episode of *The Twilight Zone. Candid Camera,* maybe? A practical joke? No—as it turns out, it was none of the above. Our music and message were having an impact in Israel…right up to the front door of the King David Hotel!

Likewise, while traveling and ministering in Israel in the spring of 2019, I was confronted with an article in the *Jerusalem Post* that stopped me in my tracks. The largest and most widely read paper in Israel featured an article in its "Diaspora" edition. ("Diaspora" refers to the dispersion of the Jews outside the Land of Israel.) The headline read: "Study: One-Fifth of Jewish Millennials Believe Jesus Is the Son of God."

This can't be right. I immediately began to argue with the headline. But what if it was even close to being right? What if the real number was more like 10 percent? That would still be a miracle we have hoped and prayed to see. I had heard in the past that perhaps there were ten to twenty thousand Jewish believers in Israel, but 20 percent of *all Jewish Millennials* is nothing short of mind-blowing.

God is at work among the Jewish people. The Church has a duty, as instructed by Jesus Himself, to care for them. Yeshua said, "I tell you the truth, when you did it for one of the least of these my brothers and sisters, you were doing it for me" (Matthew 25:40 NIV). Later in that same parable, He said, "I was naked, hungry, sick, thirsty, in prison, a stranger…and you did not look after me." Jesus clearly identifies with His Jewish people and equates a person's eternal destiny with how His brothers and sisters are treated. Why do you suppose He makes such a strong equation here? Because when Jews (or anyone else for that matter) see a Christian, they believe they are seeing Jesus. Jesus is telling those who follow Him, who say they love and worship Him, that *it is very important how you represent Me to the world. I gave My life for all of them. In fact, one of the Ten Commandments is: do not bear the Name of the Lord your God in a vain way.*

CHURCH HISTORY CHALLENGES

Back in the 1960s and 1970s, the world experienced a powerful and unique expression of heavenly grace that came to be known as the Jesus Movement. It was an amazing season for the outpouring of the Holy Spirit in preaching, teaching, evangelism, signs and wonders, miracles, and especially the conviction of sin and the need for a Savior-Redeemer. It was a global call back to the God of creation, and during those blessed days, many Jewish people, including me, were swept up in the nets of the Fisher of men's souls.

People like Oral Roberts, Kenneth Hagin, and Billy Graham became household names. Bible sales went through the roof. Churches grew by leaps and bounds, as did mission organizations, conferences, and Christian music festivals. People were getting saved in coffee shops, shopping malls, beauty parlors, and bars as the Holy Spirit breathed conviction and salvation across the globe. My turn to surrender arrived on that fishing trip in Bumpus Mills, Tennessee, on March 26, 1977, as I mentioned earlier.

During these glorious days of outpouring, many Jews like me came to faith and became passionate about sharing their love for God and our Messiah with our own Jewish people. Moishe Rosen founded Jews for Jesus in California. Messianic synagogues and congregations sprang up in Chicago, Cincinnati, Philadelphia, and Rockville, to name a few. The groundbreaking music team called Lamb, headed by my friend Joel Chernoff, and my own recording group, Israel's Hope, hit the road to worship the King of the Jews and to remind the Church and Israel that Jesus Christ is also Yeshua the Messiah, a Jewish rabbi from Nazareth.

There was great excitement for many years, but as the Jesus Movement began to wane, we found ourselves caught up in the weeds of defending our faith and practice against old doctrines and some bad church traditions that had plagued Jewish believers in the past.

For example, Ignatius, Bishop of Antioch (AD 98–117), wrote in his Epistle to the Magnesians, "For if we are still practicing Judaism, we admit that we have not received God's favor.... It is wrong to talk about Jesus Christ and live like Jews. For Christianity did not believe in Judaism, but Judaism in Christianity." This man is considered to have been a solid Christian, but I believe he was lacking in some basic understanding with regard to faith and the Jewish people. I highlight this statement because this thinking can still be found in the Church around the world today. If I were to stand in any number of pulpits in any given city in the Western world and make that same statement this afternoon, I believe I would get a rousing "Amen" and perhaps even a standing ovation.

Another such voice was Saint Jerome (AD 347–420). He was born into a pagan family in Dalmatia and became a lawyer after studying in Rome. Although he was baptized in Rome at the age of eighteen, he was reported to have had a "true conversion" later after studying the Bible. He spent most of his life in seclusion, prayer, and fasting—first in the Syrian desert, and finally for thirty years in a monastery in Bethlehem. There he translated the Hebrew and Greek Scriptures into what is known as the Latin Vulgate. It is still in use today. He seems to sum up much of the thinking of the early Church fathers with regard to the Jewish people. As quoted in *The Jewish Encyclopedia*, he said this about Jewish believers in Jesus: "While they pretend to be both Jews and Christians, they are neither."

To be candid, I don't know where to begin in the face of such comments. First, let me repeat that Jesus wasn't a Christian. He didn't preach a radical exit from the Judaism of His day; rather, He preached the Kingdom of God. He didn't speak against the Temple, the sacrifices, prayer, worship, holy days, Sabbath, or Jerusalem. He's the One who gave them in the first place to Moses, the priests, and the prophets. He did have a problem with those who preached them and didn't do them. He also had a problem with those who misused and misrepresented them for their own gain. In other words, He didn't preach against the Law or the prophets—He fulfilled them.

Second, there is a big difference between being a Jew and the religion of Judaism. Being a Jew is a matter of DNA. You don't get a choice in the matter. Oddly, the State of Israel decided to let Adolf Hitler have a say in defining who a Jew was. When the Nazis invaded countries throughout Europe, they had to decide who would be deported to the death camps and who would remain. They defined a Jew as being anyone with Jewish blood going back three generations on either side of your family tree; if that was you, it meant you were shipped away for destruction. As a result, after the war, the State of Israel decided that anyone having a Jewish grandparent on either side of the family would have the distinction of being called a Jew and afforded the right to make *aliyah* to Israel and become a naturalized citizen.

Judaism, on the other hand, is a religion. It can be practiced by anyone, no matter their genetic background. You may convert to Judaism—but one cannot convert DNA to become a Jew. The God of Abraham made a promise that was repeated to his son Isaac and to his son Jacob/Israel and to his sons. The promise was based on a bloodline because God was raising a family and building a Kingdom, not a religion.

Finally, I would ask Bishop Ignatius, "Who was grafted into whom?" Was a wild olive branch grafted into a cultivated olive tree, or was it the other way around, as he seems to indicate?

The truth of the matter, however, is that *all* our blood has been corrupted. We all need the transfusion from the Lamb of God, the Messiah of Israel, to restore us to our proper place in the Kingdom. When we come to be family together, that same precious blood of Yeshua is given freely to all who ask—making us family because we then share the same heavenly DNA. This is why Jesus said, "Unless you eat the flesh of the Son of Man and drink his blood you have no life in you" (John 6:53 NIV). Now, in the natural we retain the distinctions of Jew and Gentile, male and female, black and white, but in His Spirit, we are equal, the same. We are family, and He is not ashamed to call us brothers and sisters (Hebrews 2:11).

An Unshakable Kingdom

For many years we Messianic Jews wrestled with doctrines, traditions, and practices like the one described above. How do we as Jews live, worship, and express our faith in a way that is faithful to the One who called us and gave us breath? Many of the Jewish traditions and practices we grew up with were good: the holy days, Hebrew, the Bible, the God of our fathers, many of the prayers taken from the Psalms, circumcision, *mikveh* (baptism), Shabbat, etc. But the early Church fathers rejected much of this over the centuries, and sometimes even forbade it.

In those early days of the Messianic movement, we prayed and fasted regularly because we wanted to know from the Scriptures, and indeed from the Spirit of God, how we were to live as Jews. We longed to be faithful to the calling we had received as Jews and to worship in a way that pleased the Lord and communicated to our Jewish brethren that we were worshiping the God of Abraham, Isaac, and Jacob. We were and still are passionate about communicating the truth about Yeshua the Messiah to our own people by both declaration and demonstration.

In short, we are trying to live our lives the way Jesus lived His. We love and honor the Bible as the Word of the Living God, from Genesis to Revelation. We celebrate the special feasts and sabbaths because they help us remember the faithfulness of God in each generation. We honor and keep (to the best of our understanding) the Sabbath as it is a part of the weekly cycle of work, worship, and rest that God modeled and prescribed for us. We circumcise our male children because it is a sign of the covenant God made with our people (as Jesus did). There is more we do and don't do simply because we are a holy nation, a royal priesthood, and a people belonging to God.

We have been brought into a Kingdom that cannot be shaken. We have not simply joined another religious system that forsakes our identity and roots. Show me someone perfect in all his ways and I'll show you my Messiah. Jesus is the one we want to emulate. We want to walk like Him, talk like Him, love each other like Him, and see His Kingdom come on Earth as it is in Heaven.

In John 5:19, Yeshua makes one of my favorite statements about life: "The Son can do nothing by himself; he can do only what he sees his Father doing, because whatever the Father does the son also does" (NIV). I love this statement and have adopted it for my own life with a little twist. I can't see the Father like Jesus did, but Jesus said, "Anyone who has seen me has seen the Father" (John 14:9 NIV). So with all humility, and a bit of fear and trembling, I would like to say some day with faith: "If you have seen me, you have seen my Messiah."

Jews and Gentiles are finally being reunited. As both sides of the great sword are being drawn together at this point in history, we are drawn together at the familial healing of the table. Just as when the family joins together on the Sabbath for a holy meal of rest and fellowship before the new week, so too a new era is dawning for the Children of Abraham. We are no longer divided as we step forth into this new dawn. We are united in Yeshua and His Kingdom.

CHAPTER 9

A New Era Dawning

When it comes to reaching the Jewish people, I have a deep concern with Western Christianity. I aim to share it here as lovingly as possible, while still speaking with clarity about the challenge before us in this new era. My concern is this: Yeshua, the rabbi from Nazareth, has been methodically, and often intentionally, presented as anything but a Jewish rabbi, much less the Jewish Messiah. Why is this so important? As we saw earlier, when Israel recognizes her own Messiah it will mean salvation for the nations, life from the dead for Israel, and the Kingdom of God on Earth.

We seem to have crossed a line in the sand. Our step of faith has led us into a new time, even a new era. Jesus must remain in Heaven until the "time" to restore all things. It's a big statement, but I believe that time draws near. Through the Jacksonville encounter, the roar from Zion vision, raising the funds, writing the songs, presenting the vision, and preaching this message, I have a unique perspective on all of it.

Why should a vision or encounter like the one I described earlier be so compelling and exciting for someone like me? All my believing life I have carried the burden for Israel, my Jewish people, to see the truth about who Jesus really is. All my decades of travels, ministry, and music have been connected to one great hope—that all Israel would be saved as described in Romans 11:25–26. All my songs and recordings are infused with the hope that Jewish people will not only hear something familiar, but also experience something mostly unfamiliar—the presence of the Holy One of Israel who inhabits the praises of His people (Psalm 22:3).

I have believed that the Church would see this hope of Israel's salvation as a rallying call from Heaven, just as the Apostle Paul wrote to the Church at Rome: "I am not ashamed of the gospel, because it is the power of God that brings salvation to everyone who believes: first to the Jew, then to the Gentile" (Romans 1:16 NIV). But sadly, it didn't take very many years into my new life to realize how little understanding—and even less passion—there was in the Church to see Israel embrace her own Messiah. Such efforts were few and far between.

Mostly, I found a Church glad to hear when Jews accepted Jesus Christ and adopted a totally foreign way of worship, with people not their own, with a language that rarely mentioned the importance of Moses and the prophets. Worse yet, that Church had ignored and even replaced the sacred times God had told Israel to remember and keep forever. These were probably two good reasons why Jewish missionary groups like Jews for Judaism successfully won back so many of the "wayward flock" of Jews from Christ and back to traditional rabbinic Judaism.

As a young believer, when I would ask my evangelical brothers and sisters, "Why don't we celebrate Passover or Yom Kippur or Tabernacles?" I usually got the stock answer: "Well, Jesus fulfilled all those things." But when I probed a little deeper into what the Scriptures meant by "fulfilled," I found the answers less satisfying. Let me explain.

DISGUISING JESUS

If you hear the words of Jesus Himself speaking to a Jewish audience in Jerusalem in Matthew 23, you begin to understand the root of the problem: "For I tell you, you will not see me again, until you say, 'Blessed is he who comes in the name of the Lord'" (Matthew 23:39 NIV).

These familiar words are the traditional greeting the bride uses to welcome the bridegroom under the *chuppah*, where they cut a covenant of marriage. Jesus is saying here that the Jewish people will need to recognize Him as their Messiah and welcome Him to come and be their Bridegroom. Any self-respecting Jew knows Jerusalem will never marry a Gentile messiah, so what better way to keep Jesus from returning than by disguising their very own Bridegroom as anything but Jewish?

The best parallel for this deceitful design is hidden in the life story of Joseph, the beloved son of the patriarch Jacob, later renamed Israel. Remember that as Joseph grew up in the tents of his father, Jacob, his older brothers began to despise him for his dreams and visions. He had the favor of his father, but as a result, he had to endure the anger and resentment of his brothers to the point where they desired to kill him. Instead, they sold Joseph to a passing caravan, which in turn sold him as a slave to a wealthy Egyptian household. From there he served years of undeserved prison time until his giftings brought him before Pharaoh himself. Joseph was then elevated to the number two slot in the government, from which he saved an entire nation and the rest of the known world from a devastating seven-year drought and famine.

The story takes an interesting twist when Joseph's brothers come before his throne in Egypt in need of food for their starving families back in Canaan. Several times they presented themselves to their brother asking for assistance, but they did not recognize him even after many hours of face-to-face conversation. Why? Because Joseph was so culturally concealed as an Egyptian that even the family that had known him his entire life could not see through the disguise.

He no longer looked like a Jew. He didn't speak like a Jew. He didn't act, or even smell like a Jew. When Joseph finally revealed his true identity, his brothers wept so loudly that their voices carried far beyond the walls of the palace. The man who had saved their lives and the lives of their families and children was none other than the brother they had despised and rejected so many years before.

So I appeal to the Church: Why do we insist on keeping Jesus dressed, as it were, like an Egyptian? Sounding like an Egyptian? Eating like an Egyptian? Rejecting His own Jewish roots? I believe this habit, while unintentionally practiced, was demonically invented to keep Jesus's brothers from recognizing Him. When Israel's eyes are opened, they too "will grieve bitterly for Him as one grieves for a firstborn son" (Zechariah 12:10 NIV).

Jesus said, "For I tell you, you will not see me again until you say, 'Blessed is he who comes in the name of the Lord'" (Matthew 23:37–39 NIV). He told us that we would not see Him again until those words, which have been used at every Jewish wedding ceremony from the beginning of time, are cried out to Him from a desperate Jerusalem. I can't tell you the number of times I have sung that simple prayer over those who came to the synagogue to be married. That's what Jesus was describing. The disrobing of Jesus as a Gentile God and returning Him to His throne in Jerusalem, where He belongs, as the Lion and the Lamb, the King of the Jews, has been my passion—the point of my music, message, and ministry.

How to Remove the Disguise?

How do we take the Egyptian disguise off Joseph and the Greek-god illusion off Yeshua? We are in a major time of restoration, as Peter spoke about in Acts 3. What would happen if the Church decided to restore a biblical calendar for the major celebrations of the King and understanding the Hebraic context for our preaching and teaching? What if the Jewish people were seen as partners of salvation? What if Christians could have more of a sense of gratitude and compassion towards the rabbis and synagogues with the understanding that we all worship the God of Abraham, Isaac, and Jacob? What if we actively remembered that if it weren't for God's faithfulness through the Jewish people none of us would have the fear or knowledge of God? What if the *Moedim*, the appointed times or holy days, were restored to the Church calendar with deep understanding that they all speak of the work of Jesus and His life and ministry?

I have heard many times from New Covenant scholars that unless we think like first-century Jews we will not understand a huge portion of what the apostles wrote about in the gospels, much less the writings of Paul. There are countless treasures to be unearthed in the Hebrew language when coupled with the traditions and experiences of religious Jewish life.

Did you ever stop to wonder why Jesus was transfigured with Moses and Elijah on the mountain top? Was it because He was displacing them and their words and ministries? Or could it be that He was pointing to them as messengers of truth whose words still have value today when understood through His life? I propose that we are drawing close to a revelation. Just as Jesus was transformed before His disciples in the company of Moses and Elijah, so too will we be transformed when He returns and stands on the Mount of Olives in Jerusalem.

We see evidence of this coming revelation in the political-cultural realm as well. In 1988, exactly forty years after Ben-Gurion's declaration of Israeli independence, a group of Messianic Jewish pioneers (including me) organized a worldwide conference to be held in Jerusalem during the fortieth anniversary of the rebirth of the State of Israel. This conference not only commemorated Israel's birthday, but was held during the celebration of Shavuot, the Feast of Pentecost. It had been more than 1,900 years since the world had seen a large group of Jewish believers in Jesus celebrating the Feast in Jerusalem (see Acts 2).

Before we knew it, we were looking for a hotel in the city with room for a thousand worshipers from all over the world. But we soon discovered that the city's hotels did not share our enthusiasm. In fact, they all turned us away. In order to run a hotel or operate a restaurant in Israel, a Kosher certificate is needed—and the rabbis would gladly pull the license of any establishment giving Jewish believers in Jesus a place to hold a conference.

Our conference was to begin on Erev Shabbat (Friday night), continue all day on the Sabbath, and conclude Sunday night, after the Feast of Shavuot/Pentecost. It looked as if our vision for the event was dead in the water.

But God.

As it happened, the first Palestinian Intifada (Arab uprising) had begun five months earlier. It became so violent and intense that many Jewish pilgrims and tourists stayed out of the country during Shavuot despite the fact that it was Israel's fortieth birthday. On the far-east side of Jerusalem, right on the so-called "Green Line," which marked the demilitarized Palestinian-occupied portion of Israel, stood a hotel large enough to house us all and which was in severe financial straits— the Diplomat. The staff didn't seem to care who we were or what we believed. Money talked in east Jerusalem.

So we filled not only the Diplomat, but also a small boutique hotel a few steps away called Eden. The Diplomat even put a huge sign over the front door reading, "Welcome Messianic Jews Conference Shavuot '88." In case anyone didn't read English, they printed it in Hebrew as well.

We made great use of the hotel for two and a half days, worshiping and praying together until 3:00 a.m. in the restaurant, rooms, and on the grounds anytime we wished. But even though we were passionate in prayer, worship, and our pursuit of His presence, no one ever said they saw tongues of fire dancing on our heads or Heaven opening with angels coming and going. Nevertheless, we all admitted that the sense of His presence was pure and powerful.

A tremendous feeling of joy and ecstasy filled everyone present. We all left happy, spiritually encouraged, and satisfied that we had heard and obeyed the call to go to Jerusalem for the feast. But it would take another thirty years to see with our own eyes and hear with our own ears the fullness of the reason we had been called there.

The decision to move the American Embassy from Tel Aviv to Jerusalem, known as the "Jerusalem Embassy Act of 1995," was adopted by the United States Senate during the Clinton administration with a vote of 93–5 and by the House of Representatives with a vote of 374–37. The Act became law without a presidential signature on November 8, 1995—and yet the American embassy remained exactly where it was until Donald Trump came into office and made it happen in 2018. Why was that?

It started when the United States placed its energy dependence in the hands of the oil-rich Arab states of the Middle East. As we all know, the Arabs and the Israelis have not exactly had the warmest relationship on the planet. For centuries, the Arab states had been plotting Israel's demise should she ever become a nation again. So despite agreeing to move the American Embassy in 1995, our leaders cited national security as the reason for postponing it. Keeping the Arab power brokers happy was foremost in American minds. They controlled how much oil flowed to any nation, thereby controlling the price—and whoever controls the power grid controls the economy and financial health of that nation. So for more than twenty years, no president had the *chutzpah* (that's Yiddish for "nerve") to upset them.

I have heard in my spirit for many years that embassy moves were coming among the nations. I sensed the need to watch carefully which of them made the move to Jerusalem and when. I believe the Spirit of God spoke to me about it and said, "Watch the nations for the movement of their embassies. Those who make the move will be marked as Sheep nations, and those who refuse will be marked as Goat nations. And the one that moves first, I will bless abundantly."

I began to watch, pray, and preach this message in nations where I believed I had the liberty to share it, hoping all the while that the United States of America would have the courage to claim the prize. I shared these words many times in Latin America, as I found there a great love for God, the Jewish people, and Israel. I also knew that those countries were the last to move their embassies out of Jerusalem, so they might be the first to return.

Then came 2016. To say the least, the political climate in America during the presidential election cycle was a wild ride. I had become much more involved in the national political scene because of my concern for our society, our culture, and what my children and grand-children would be inheriting. I was concerned about what would happen if the voice of righteousness were to simply leave the govern-ment to the same forces that empowered Ahab and Jezebel. I encour-aged people everywhere I went to pray and vote their conscience. I reminded them that righteousness in leadership would bring the blessing of God on our nation, while sin and unrighteousness were a reproach to any people (Proverbs 14:34).

I believed that any Bible-toting, born-again, Jesus-loving Christian would agree with my call for righteousness and moral clarity. Who in their right mind would argue against Israel's right to exist within secure, defensible borders, a defenseless baby's right to live inside the womb, or the God-given right to life, liberty, and the pursuit of hap-piness for any human being on the planet no matter their race, color, or creed? I received many thank yous along the way, but I also was treated to lots of pushback for being "too political or controversial."

I have never understood the intensity of the controversy around the Jewish State's right to exist in the Middle East, to have Jews occupy their ancient homeland. The courage required of an individual to stand on principle of conscience and do the right thing is one thing, but for an entire nation to do the same takes the courage of a lion and a leader with a moral compass grounded in the Word of God. In modern times, that list is very short and distinguished, including Harry S. Truman, Winston Churchill, Ronald Reagan, and now, in my opinion, you can add the name of Donald J. Trump.

The whole world began to buzz when he announced his decision to move the American embassy to Jerusalem. To make such a bold and possibly disastrous move drew the criticism of many members of his own government, foreign leaders, and mainstream media across the globe. I, on the other hand, was ecstatic. I really believed what I had heard in the Spirit. I was excited to see what it might mean for both the United States and Israel.

Israel received the news with great joy and appreciation. There was only one great task left to seal the deal: to find the place for the embassy to be built.

The search was on. Jerusalem is a tightly packed city with very little real estate available in the size and shape that would be needed to house the U.S. Embassy and Consulate. Because land is scarce, Jerusalem is the most expensive city in the world in which to develop real estate.

After months of searching, two buildings became available on the far-east side of Jerusalem that could meet the needs of the American people: the same two hotels where my friends and ministry partners and I had met to pray for Israel years before!

That's right: The United States government purchased the Diplomat and Eden hotels in May 2018, on the seventieth anniversary of Israel's birth, during the Feast of Shavuot or Pentecost, and thirty years almost to the day after we Messianic Jews had spent three days worshiping and praying for a visitation and a miracle. I still smile every time I think of how the prayers of a small group of people may have influenced the future of two nations.

It is also interesting that the number seventy is associated with the Hebrew letter *ayin*. When it is printed in its ancient form, this Hebrew letter looks like an open eye and, as I mentioned earlier, is interpreted as "seeing." So in the seventieth year, the year of the *ayin*, President Trump honored the God of Israel by declaring Jerusalem the eternal and undivided capital of Israel and moved the U.S. embassy to the hotels that had been prayed over and sanctified so many years ago.

UNDERSTANDING THE MYSTERY

The restoration and fullness of the Ecclesia and the salvation of Israel have always been a major theme of my life and prayers, the double-edged sword. Again, as the Apostle Paul wrote to the early Roman Church, we need each other in order to see and hear:

> I do not want you to be ignorant of this mystery brothers, so that you may not be conceited: Israel has experienced a hardening [blindness] in part until the full number [fullness] of the Gentiles has come in. And so, all Israel will be saved.... (Romans 11:25–26 NIV)

Those are provocative words, to say the least. Those words have been debated, preached, and dissected to find their true meaning ever since the Apostle Paul penned them to the fledgling church at Rome as early as AD 57.

The two words in brackets in the quotation above are not my own. They are translated as such by many standard translations, but not in my beloved NIV. In this new time, I am seeing these two verses, and many others, in a different light.

Let's start with the word "mystery." This is generally understood to be something difficult or maybe even impossible to understand or explain. I would add that it is something that needs to be uncovered, explained, or revealed by wisdom or revelation. Paul even tells the Romans that he is about to uncover a mystery so that the Gentiles won't live their entire lives in conceit. Let me paraphrase his next statement with a passage I quoted earlier:

> The Jewish people have experienced a partial blindness, or a hardening of their hearts to the reality that Yeshua is the Messiah, until the *pleromatos* of the Gentiles has been revealed and demonstrated in the Kingdom.

The word in italics is the Greek word translated as "fullness" in most of our modern translations, or "the full number" (NIV). My Greek study guide lists several meanings that can be interpreted from this word, so it seems translators could have a theological bias or slant one way or the other. First, *pleromatos* can be defined as a "quantity of being," as in the fullness or abundance of a measure, meaning "a number or an accounting of something." This is the tack NIV translators took with this verse. Second, and much more to my sense, it can be defined as a "quality of existence" as in "the fullness of divine perfections; a state of fullness or abundance of blessing."

Herein lie the differing opinions concerning the mystery about which Paul is speaking. Do the "blindness or the hardening in part" that have been imposed upon Israel await *a full number* of Gentiles to be counted among the righteous? Or do they await *a quality of condition* of the Gentile church to remove the scales so Israel can see her own promised Messiah?

I have a strong opinion on this question, and my conclusion is based on yet another passage that contains this same word, *pleromatos*. Let's look at a very well-known and often-discussed verse that Jesus mentioned during the famous Sermon on the Mount. In Matthew's gospel, Yeshua says this:

> Do not think that I have come to abolish [destroy] the Law or the Prophets. I have not come to abolish them, but to fulfill [*plero'o*] them. I tell you the truth, until Heaven and earth disappear, not the smallest letter, nor the least stroke of a pen, will by any means disappear from the Law until everything is accomplished. (Matthew 5:17–18 NIV)

Again, we encounter this word, "fulfill." I have included the Greek transliteration so we can see it is the same root word used by Paul in Romans 11, but in another form. The English translation for this form of *pleromatos* remains pretty much the same: "to fill full to an abundance, impart richly, fully supplied, made perfect." And just so we won't be tempted to say the word "fulfill" here—meaning "complete," as in done-away with, discarded, finished, and on to a new task—Jesus says the fullness of the Law and the prophets should be taught as He teaches and demonstrates it, not ignored.

Now with these two passages and this common word "fulfill" as the linking premise, I propose something for the Ecclesia to consider. Could it be that the salvation of Israel and the revelation of Jesus as Messiah is linked to a fullness—an abundance of divine perfection as demonstrated by a restored and revived servant Gentile body known as the Church?

I can hear some of the conversations at a synagogue already:

Did you hear what's happening down the street at that church where there's a line to get into the services? They celebrate Shabbat just like us. They light the candles. They do the Hebrew blessings, take *Kiddish*—they call it communion—and read the Torah. The worship music is from the Psalms and prophets, and the singing is beautiful and passionate. They love each other and pray for each other's needs, saying *Shabbat shalom* and meaning it.

They celebrate the holidays and fast on Yom Kippur. They gave up Easter eggs and do a Passover seder instead with such deep love and understanding that I got completely lost in it. Many of them have put a *mezuzah* on their doorposts and say El Shaddai is now the owner and guardian of their homes.

These Gentiles say they love the God of Abraham, Isaac, and Jacob, and even us. And I'm starting to believe them!

My sister went down there last Shabbat with her Christian friend from work and said she heard a strong message against antisemitism and a strong prayer of support for Israel and the Jewish community here in town. They prayed for people who then got well. They prayed for our Temple and the rest of our city.

What in the world is going on there? All my life I was told these people hated us and would eventually turn on us just like every other nation. *Maybe times have changed?*

Just imagine it.

Remember the quote I shared earlier from Rabbi Yoel Schwartz in Jerusalem? "Messiah will be revealed when nations (Gentiles) keep the Sabbath." How do you suppose the Messiah will "be revealed"? Will it be as a passing cloud that looks like a man, or in the demonstration of a Church that loves and embraces the fullness of Israel's Messiah?

EARS TO HEAR

Several years ago, after a concert in a large city in Texas, my host told me a local conservative rabbi had asked if I would go to his synagogue the next morning for a meeting. Of course I agreed, wondering what to expect. It happened to be a Sunday morning, so the synagogue parking lot was completely empty when my host and I arrived, except for one car that I presumed was the rabbi's. The massive double doors to the entrance were open, so we let ourselves into the beautiful, spacious entryway. No receptionist or signs directed us to the rabbi's office, but I thought I heard the strains of familiar music somewhere in the distant hallways.

We followed the sounds, and sure enough, they led us to another set of massive wooden doors and the music. Two strong knocks on the doors, and the music came to an immediate halt, followed by a booming voice: "Come in." An imposing figure of a man rose from behind his desk to greet us. I instantly thought, *This must be what Tevye (from* Fiddler on the Roof) *would look like in person.*

We spoke cordially for a few minutes, and then the rabbi shocked me by turning his TV monitor to face me. He had been watching a video of "Shalom Jerusalem"—that classic night of worship and praise from the convention center in downtown Jerusalem in 1995. His next words almost knocked me off my chair: "Would you consider coming here to my synagogue and teaching us how to worship Adonai again?"

Traditionally, Jews have been excluded from worshiping in the Church unless they are transformed to worship like Christians. Such an approach ignores the Jewish personality, the perspectives on the Torah, and the foundations of the faith. How can we expect the Jewish community to pay any attention to the Gospel when we, as the Church, ignore the testimony of Moses, the Law, and the prophets? Moses is the prophet until the appearance of Jesus the Messiah. When Jesus returns, He's actually going to be sitting on a throne in Jerusalem—the real Jerusalem, right there in the middle of that little country. Then the millennium, the thousand-year reign of Christ, will take place. That's what's coming.

Unfortunately, I think a lot of Christians will be playing catch-up between now and then. And what is the very first item on King Yeshua's agenda when He returns? He will oversee the very first international celebration of the Feast of Tabernacles in Jerusalem (Zechariah 14). The understanding of all these things, that the Kingdom is both here and not yet, has fueled this movement of restoration and the Roar from Zion. Heaven is calling; do we have ears to hear?

CHAPTER 10

TASTE AND SEE

No one can deny the following statement: *Times are changing.* As I shared in the chapter about Pastor Stovall's encounter, even mature believers, men and women, pastors and elders have been challenged to think, pray, and seek to understand with a new set of eyes and ears. It has taken months and even years for some to process what the Lord was telling us back in March 2018.

Today many people still ask compelling questions. Maybe you do too:

- How do I approach some of the things I am hearing from the pulpit when they seem so different from what I thought before?
- Am I hearing sound doctrine, or is this simply an emotional response to a spiritual experience?

- How do I go about implementing some of the things
related to the reunification of Jewish and Gentile
believers, restoring God's Kingdom family on Earth as
it is in Heaven?

My answer is simple: *Taste and see.* How do you do that? By going back to the basics. In the rest of this chapter, I will outline several practical ways you can engage with what God is doing in the world right now. Don't take my word for it. Taste and see for yourself.

BACK TO THE BASICS

When I was a brand-new believer in 1977, I asked the same questions some of you may be asking right now. I had an advantage over many because I had a model to watch and imitate: Jerry—the young man who had introduced me to the Presence of the Lord. He kept a small NIV New Testament in his back pocket all the time and often quoted the Scriptures to me, and we prayed together often. From Jerry I not only learned of the true grandeur of the Lord and the salvation of the Messiah, but also valuable lessons about how to know if what I was hearing, seeing, and speaking were really aligned with God's Word.

Here is a short list of basics Jerry taught me that will help anyone understand and discern if what they are hearing is the truth or a deception:

1. *Make reading your Bible a daily habit, not an occasional
   investment.* The Bible is our source for hearing the voice
   of God. In it we discover with certainty what He thinks
   and what is true. It is sharper than any two-edged sword

and divides between lies and the truth. When understood and interpreted for us through the Holy Spirit, it
can lead us into *all* truth and keep us from being snared
by mere teachings of men. If it is written in your Bible,
you can be certain God said it. There may be differing
opinions or interpretations of some aspects, but the truth
of God's Word stands forever.

2. *Pray to converse with the Living God.* The Apostle Paul
told us to "pray without ceasing" (1 Thessalonians 5:17
NIV). Jesus spent untold hours each day in prayer speaking with His Father and being refreshed even after
spending an entire day of ministry surrounded by needy
crowds of people. Prayer refreshes and provides information, instruction, training, and discipline. In prayer our
lives can be reordered, and our thoughts can be changed
in a moment by a supernatural download. Many times,
I have been instructed about my future and directed by
the Lord from an impression on my heart or even the
leading of the Holy Spirit for a future plan. The closeness
of the Spirit of God in prayer is a reward that brings peace
and confidence for the day or the task ahead.

3. *Fast with prayer.* Some people think fasting is simply a
method by which you prove to God you are really serious about a request you made. Fasting is not a hunger
strike to force God's hand to do something for you; it is
for us. Many voices vie for our attention every day—the
voice of man, the world, our own flesh, the temptations
of the enemy, and the voice of God. One great tool
Heaven has given us to filter out the cacophony of

distraction is fasting. Denying yourself food is one sure way to let your flesh know it is not in control. When your mind finally stops screaming at you to stop at the next Burger King, it is much easier to hear the word of God.

Early in my walk with Jesus, I had plenty of desires and bad habits that needed to be conquered by the Spirit of God, so I began fasting one day each week. The combination of reading my Bible daily, prayer, and weekly fasting made me nearly unrecognizable to my old self in just a few weeks. In Matthew 6:16, Jesus says, *"When you fast,"* not *"if you fast."* In Matthew 17:21, Jesus casts out an evil spirit from a young boy His disciples had no power over. He told His disciples that "this kind only comes out by prayer and fasting."

4. *Memorize the Scriptures.* Proverbs 23:7 says, "As a man thinks within himself, so is he" (TPT). The fastest and most effective way to see change in your life is to change your thought process—and the quickest and most effective way I know to change the way you think is to memorize the Scriptures. Early in my Christian walk, I embarked on a methodical pattern of memorizing the verses that spoke loudest to me. At first it was just a simple, short verse, but then I became addicted as I saw the power these words had to change my thoughts, words, and even the desires of my heart. Eventually, I found myself memorizing entire chapters. Those many hours spent memorizing the Word of God have served me well and have continued to speak to me throughout my entire life.

5. *Giving.* If we see giving as simply a means for the church to pay its bills and staff, we will miss out on the real power of it. There are really only two types of exchange in our self-focused world—buying and selling. We expect to get what we pay for, and if we don't, we get frustrated. The Kingdom of God operates on a completely separate system that Jesus calls *sowing and reaping.* This system is built on a relationship and covenant, and the results are apparent.

The Parable of the Sower shows this most clearly in Matthew 13, Mark 4, and Luke 8. This principle of sowing and reaping is so important to understanding how the Kingdom works that Jesus says, "If you don't understand this, you will not understand anything about the Kingdom." Sowing is also much more than just finances. We sow time in prayer, serving others, giving of our food or clothing, and sharing whatever is needed in the lives of people. When a farmer sows one kernel of corn in his field, he can expect in time to reap thousands of kernels in return. This kingdom principle really works, but it is also connected with the all-important covenant relationship.

1. *Fellowship of family and faith.* The author of Hebrews warns us not to give up meeting together as some are in the habit of doing, but to encourage one another—and all the more as we see the Day approaching. In this current era of COVID-19, when some governments limit our ability to meet and encourage one another, how much more important does practicing Shabbat in our homes become? Consider that perhaps the Lord already

knew this was coming and began to prepare us for it with the restoration of worship in our homes with the Shabbat for the people of God.

2. *Service.* Serving one another and our world is another way the Kingdom provides us with context for declaring and demonstrating the goodness of God and His love for us all. Haven't you ever heard someone tell of an opportunity to serve where he received much more than he gave? Did you notice the joy and excitement on his face? It's no coincidence. It's all about sowing and reaping, covenant and Kingdom. I encourage you to find some area to serve your community of faith.

THE VOICE OF THE FATHER

Earlier I demonstrated that there's a movement afoot in which God is restoring the voice of the Father to His people. We now see a call for integrity in ministry and responsibility and accountability with gifts like teaching and prophecy. We are experiencing liberty in our churches to really worship the way Israel worshiped those many centuries ago. Today we see the Church reacting tremendously, yet cautiously, to a lot of the things that have been prophesied regarding a restoration of the demonstration of the Kingdom.

The Kingdom starts on page one of our Bibles and goes all the way through the final "Amen." We must change our perspective from a faith that only embraces Matthew through the Revelation of John. We must stop acting as if two-thirds of God's infallible Word just passed away and is simply there for historical reference. I like the saying that the New is in the Old concealed, and the Old is in the New revealed.

The entire Word of God is like a strong fortress. There are foundations beneath, upon which the entire structure is built. The Law and the prophets are the foundation upon which the New Covenant in Jesus and the teachings of the Apostles are built. (Read Matthew 5–7 carefully, and you will see what I am saying here.)

We must start by acknowledging and wrestling with the foundation of the Church. We must look into the Scriptures and see the same God moving throughout all of history, moving poetically as He tells the grand story of creation, redemption, and restoration.

In John 5:19, Jesus was defending himself against the Pharisees after He healed the paralyzed man. "Jesus gave them this answer: 'Very truly I tell you, the Son can do nothing by himself; he can do only what he sees his Father doing, because whatever the Father does the Son also does" (John 5:19 NIV). In other words, Yeshua tells them that children pattern their lifestyles after their fathers. And in John 8:44, He rebukes some zealous religious hypocrites for being "murderers from the beginning," just like their father, the devil. If we are the children and family of Yahweh, we will listen to the Father and learn from Him. Our lifestyles, desires, ambitions, hopes, dreams, needs, wants, thoughts, words, and deeds will all reflect the Father.

Are you ready for a bold life goal? Here's mine: I want to be able to say, "If you have seen me, you have seen my Messiah." You might say, "You aim too high, my brother." Well, my Bible says we have been made in His image and likeness (Genesis 1:27) and that "the Spirit of him who raised Jesus from the dead dwells in you" (Romans 8:11 ESV). And in John 17:22, Jesus declares that He has given us the "same glory" (the manifest presence of God) that the Father gave Him so that we would be one family, Jew and Gentile, demonstrating the same love and power that Jesus did and still does today through the power of the Holy Spirit.

MAKE USE OF REMINDERS

God knows we need reminders, and a lot of them. From the Fall of Man to the return of the Messiah, the Bible is filled with numerous reminders about following the Lord and His ways, how much He loves us, and how we can demonstrate that love to others. The foremost reminders are visible throughout the Sabbath and the holy days the Father provided. These appointed times provide us with a wonderful way to learn more about what God did for His people. They act as a seasonal system or spiritual calendar for remembering and honoring the Lord. Following this calendar gives us a deeper, more complete understanding of the whole story and our part in it. In Leviticus 23, the Lord spoke to Moses about these appointed times. It is interesting to note that the first listed is Shabbat, and then the passage continues to discuss the other "Feasts of the Lord" at length. So as you consider how to taste and see, let's follow the same pattern.

The concept of seventh-day rest is prominent throughout the entire Bible. In fact, it is one of the central themes. Jesus Himself observed the Sabbath. He even referred to Himself as the "Lord of the Sabbath" (Matthew 12:1–8). This is a model for us.

The Sabbath is not meant to be a burden, but a gift. We have liberty to celebrate and genuinely enjoy our time on the Sabbath. However, it's not a day to do just anything. It is a free gift offered to us to spend simply enjoying the life God has given us with the people we love.

You can remember the Sabbath with your family or group of friends in your home. A sacred meal during a special, set-apart time was the foundational expression of faith in the early Church. When we partake in communion during Shabbat, we remember Yeshua and renew the covenant He made with us in His body and blood. We recognize that He is present with us. Sabbath communion is also a prophetic anticipation of the return of King Jesus, when He will establish His eternal kingdom and we will partake with Him in the marriage supper of the Lamb (Revelation 19).

Shabbat begins with a communion dinner at sundown on Friday evening and concludes at sundown on Saturday evening every week. To welcome the Shabbat, we light two candles—one representing the light of creation and the other Jesus, as the Light of the World. Typically, a woman lights the two candles to commemorate the fact that it was through a woman that this Light came into the world. Wine (or grape juice) represents the blood of Jesus. The bread is either challah (the braided bread) or matzo (a large, unleavened cracker) that represents the body of Jesus.

In a traditional Jewish home, these same elements have different meanings, of course; but our hope is that by sharing our table on Shabbat, Jewish eyes will be opened as well. Remember the two travelers on the road to Emmaus in Luke 24? They walked with the risen Messiah for several miles while He explained the scripture verses concerning His identity. But it wasn't until they sat with Him and broke the bread that their eyes were opened and they saw Him for who He was. That's the power of the table.

Once the meal is prepared and the family is gathered, the candles are kindled, and the day of rest and fellowship begins. In our home, my wife lights the candles and invites the presence of Yeshua, the Lord of the Sabbath. I then share the bread and the cup with prayer and thanksgiving as we remember the New Covenant in the body and blood of Yeshua. Next, I offer prayers for all who are gathered around our table and sometimes share a brief Bible verse or encouraging word. Then the feast begins, and we enjoy an amazing evening of food, fellowship, and family. When we engage the Scriptures fully with open eyes, we witness the power and value of these holy days of the Lord. If you would like to see how we celebrate Shabbat, join us every week at 7:00 p.m. EST online (at WilburMinistries.com) or download our Wilbur Ministries app for free in the App Store.

PRIESTS IN OUR HOMES

Perhaps now we can see the Sabbath and all the other feasts in a different way. I don't see them as a religious responsibility, but rather as a demonstration of a covenantal relationship where we set apart the time, invite the Bridegroom, and celebrate the covenant He made with us. At the table, Mom and Dad have an opportunity to be priests of the New Covenant in their own home. We pray, invite the Lord to join us, remember Yeshua's sacrifice with the challah and the cup, feast with our family and friends, and enjoy sweet fellowship with Jesus, the Lord of the Sabbath.

I see so much of the intentions of God for us and our homes each time we gather to remember the Sabbath and keep it. Parents learn what it means to be priests in their own home as they pray, invite the presence of God, and share their table and provision with others. They pray for one another, honor the presence of the Lord, and prepare a place of reverence and honor for Him right there in the kitchen or the dining room. Now their home becomes a sanctuary.

At the table there is no hierarchy, none greater or lesser, no superior race or gender or generation. Jesus Himself is the Lord of the feast and He alone takes preeminence. We take our time to look deeply into our family's eyes and enjoy the love that binds us together—even if those sharing our table are not immediate kin. I can think of no greater display of God's love to provoke weary and disappointed hearts to surrender to the Lover of their souls. We have seen this love arrest more than one guest at our table, and I pray there are many more.

COVENANT RELATIONSHIPS

All of the basics above are powerful tools given to us that we might live a blessed and victorious life. Please don't misunderstand that last statement to mean that if you do all these things there will be no pressures or challenges in your life. I am saying that if you put the basics into practice, you will be well prepared to face every challenge that comes your way. However, none of these tools stands on its own; each is dependent on and strengthened by covenant relationships.

A few years back, my dear friend Asher Intrater wrote a book titled *Covenant Relationships* (Destiny Image, 1989). It is used in many Bible schools around the globe, and I highly recommend it. Relationships come in all forms, but covenant relationships are the deepest and weightiest of them all.

A covenant is often known as a "blood covenant" because it is initiated through the shedding of blood. To violate its terms requires the death of the offender. It was first initiated by God Himself and goes all the way back to the Garden of Eden. When Adam and Eve broke the covenant of friendship with YHVH, blood was required to satisfy the agreement. So God slew a lamb instead of killing them and covered Adam and Eve with the blood-soaked skin in atonement. We see this pattern again in Genesis 22 with Abraham and Isaac on the mountain. Ultimately, we see Yeshua as the Lamb of God whose self-sacrifice pays for the sins of the entire world.

The word "covenant" in Hebrew is *brit*. It means "to cut where blood flows." Without going too deeply into the traditions of making a covenant relationship, we begin to see the need to offer sacrifices at the Tabernacle and the Temple of God in Jerusalem. All of us have sinned and have fallen short of the glory of God, or the high standards of a relationship with God. Under the Old Covenant, there was a need for sin offerings, guilt offerings, fellowship offerings, and more in order to satisfy the demands of being in a covenant relationship with YHVH.

Nothing about the need for blood has changed in thousands of years. The only difference from the altar in Solomon's Temple and today is that the only blood acceptable to YHVH is the blood of His Son, our Messiah, Jesus of Nazareth.

Marriage is a blood covenant as well, and we can hear that in the traditional vows of "until death do us part." In the ancient world, the ring finger was not covered with a gold ring, but rather an incision was made there on the man and the woman, and then some ashes from the animal sacrifice were rubbed into the wounds to create a permanent mark to declare that person's life was already given to another. The price for adultery was the shedding of blood for breaching the strongest covenant relationship on Earth.

I have come to see the Passover celebration as a betrothal offer from God to His people Israel, and the Law at Mount Sinai as a marriage covenant between Heaven and Earth.

CONNECT THE NETS

We're hearing a lot these days about a "Billion Soul Harvest"—a mass influx of people, Jews and Gentiles alike, running to the Kingdom. If we truly are better together and have seen insurmountable evidence that the Kingdom is moving and the children of the Father are uniting, why would we not invest our all to prepare for this potential harvest?

As fishers of men, we're going to need a lot more than just one fishing boat and one net for this movement. In Luke 5, we read about Simon Peter, James, and John, who had fished all night and yet caught nothing. Jesus appeared and told Peter to cast out into the deep and throw the nets over the other side of the boat. The result of obeying Jesus was a catch so large that their nets began to break. They needed the help of their friends to haul in the supernatural catch. Today, we're talking about ways of doing the very same thing—connecting our nets to prepare for the coming supernatural harvest.

Now is the time to activate and demonstrate the Kingdom by joining our nets together, rather than simply strengthening our own. It's a Kingdom concept, not a denominational agenda. Denominations, unfortunately, are often committed to only doing things their own way. Denominationalism raises its own banner and divides rather than unites. I'm not saying denominations are inherently bad, but that there's a danger in dividing ourselves further and focusing on our differences rather than our family resemblances.

Something we need to realize in this new era is that we are now hearing from the Messiah as He stands on Heaven's shores, calling for us to prepare the harvest of His children that will overwhelm our singular vessels, the Church and the Synagogue. We have to combine our strength to be ready.

What could that look like? We're demonstrating that in a real way as Celebration Church and Wilbur Ministries have connected our nets as partnered ministries. We're lending strength to strength. We are truly better together. And we are calling out to other boats and shores to strengthen their nets and link up with ours in an effort called the Alliance. We are learning how to resource one another to fulfill the tasks each is called to do.

BE A WITNESS

A final way we can taste and see is to simply do what Jesus said when He instructed His disciples to "be my witnesses in Jerusalem and in all Judea and Samaria, and to the end of the earth" (Acts 1:8 ESV). A witness is simply someone who faithfully testifies to what he has seen and heard. Remember the Ten Commandments? One of them says: *Do not take the name of the Lord your God in vain.* Put another way, do not demonstrate to the world something that YHVH is not. He's not a liar, so don't lie. He's not a thief, so don't hold on to things that don't belong to you.

Being a witness means bearing the name of the Lord in a worthy manner. My kids reminded me of that one day years ago when I was driving. I got so angry after being cut off on the highway that I responded by catching up to the other driver, flashing my lights, and honking my horn. One of my sons said to me, "That's good, Dad. They are probably thinking right now, 'That guy must be a follower of Jesus.'" Talk about convicting!

Not bearing the Lord's name in vain is not simply a matter of avoiding saying things like "gosh darn it." It *can* be verbal, but most often it is about demonstrating through our actions that we are followers of Jesus. It's the most powerful evangelism tool we have. We show our allegiance to Jesus by how we live, how we treat the waitress at a restaurant, or what we say to someone living on the street as we walk by. After all, what are we saying if we're not demonstrating the name of the Lord? If I am not praying for the sick, I'm telling people, *I don't believe God heals.* And if I'm not sharing my bread with the needy, I'm telling people, *God is stingy. It's all about me. I worship God because of what I get.*

In this era of restoration of the Kingdom, we must carry ourselves as image bearers of the King. We are His ambassadors in this foreign land.

RESTORING THE KINGDOM

The time for the restoration of the Kingdom is upon us. As I have shown all throughout this book, YWVH is calling *all* His children together once more. Our role in this restoration process is simple: The Church must showcase the wonder of the Messiah to the world and especially to the Jewish people. We can achieve this by engaging in the appointments Heaven has provided to us all in the Scriptures, by praying for our Jewish brethren for the glory of their own Messiah to be revealed to them, by speaking the truth in love to our brothers, by welcoming them into our homes for special times and celebrations, and by literally inviting them to the table as our brothers and sisters in Christ Jesus to enjoy family, covenant, and shalom.

Quite simply, the Kingdom united is entirely indivisible, especially when you consider that if God is for us, then who can be against us or tear us apart? We must return to the whole Word of God with new eyes and see the value of being one family—the family of God made up of Jews and Gentiles who worship the God of Abraham, Moses, David, Elijah, and yes, *Yeshua, Jesus the Messiah.* We are better together, but in order to see the Jewish people enjoying their own Messiah at the table of covenant, the Church must take the first step.

You can take that first step by loving your God enough to get past old feelings, prejudices, and fear. The Church of Jesus is supposed to be a fishing boat, not a luxury liner, an ambassador of the Kingdom and not a judge of people, a bridge builder and not one who resurrects the middle wall of partition that was destroyed by the Lamb of God who took away offense and fear and condemnation. Come on, Church! I dare you to trust Jesus enough that He can reveal Yeshua and His love for His brethren after the flesh through you.

And to my Jewish people, I also invite you to taste and see. I dare you! I dare you to ask God to show you if this Yeshua is the Messiah. I know it might go against the grain of what you've been taught, and maybe even what you feel. You've been told Jesus was a deceiver, that He's a false prophet, that He lied to Israel, and that He was crucified, but He wasn't resurrected. *It was a big hoax, right?* Well, I dare you. Taste and see. Ask God to show you if it is true or not.

To the Church, I say that the Kingdom of God is so much bigger and more exciting than what we have preached it to be. Our people don't need another good sermon (though those are important, of course). They need to experience the King and the Kingdom personally. I dare you to start holding prayer meetings in your own home. I dare you to give God time to speak in your praise and worship services. I dare you to allow the gifts of the Spirit to begin to be used in the assembly. Taste and see.

No doubt some, perhaps even much, of what you've read in these pages may be new or even rub you the wrong way. It may go against what you've been taught before, whether Jew or Gentile. Now is your chance to try these "new" (actually older and traditional) teachings and discover for yourself if there's any legitimacy to them. But I warn you, once you begin to see, the world will treat you differently. Your perspective of His Kingdom will fundamentally change.

Ask the Father to reveal the truth to you. Ask for the revelation of the Spirit to wash your eyes of the blindness, to be open to the truth and the Kingdom, and to see. Let's ask the Holy Spirit to breathe on us again and to remove the planks from our eyes so we can help our brothers get the specks out of theirs.

It all starts with a prayer to the Father, a request to the King: *Let me see. Open the eyes to my heart that I may see your Kingdom and taste your blessings.* That's all it takes to start the journey. He is ready to reveal the Kingdom to you.

Will you give your all in service to the King? Will you endeavor to honor the Lord your God and love, as Yeshua put it, the least of these? Are you ready to join me in the work of building His Blackbird? The mission is clear, and we cannot fail, for "if God is for us who can be against us?" (Romans 8:31 NIV).

> The harvest is ready. Multitudes in the valley of decision. For the Day of the Lord is near.... The Lord will thunder from Jerusalem, and He will ROAR from Zion. (Joel 3:14–16 NIV)

CHAPTER 11

UNITED WE STAND

A s King David gathered all the wealth and materials necessary for building the first Temple to YHVH, he praised the Lord in the sight of the entire assembly of Israel. Then he prayed a sad prayer of thanksgiving: "We are foreigners and strangers in your sight, as were all our ancestors. Our days on earth are like a shadow, without hope" (1 Chronicles 29:15 NIV).

Is it possible David's statement of living without hope as aliens and strangers is due to the knowledge of being made in the *image* of the God of Israel, but without the hope or power to be made into His *likeness*? The writer of the Book of Hebrews tells us that our ancestors knew and admitted they were aliens and strangers on the earth. They were looking for a country of their own, a city whose architect and builder was the Lord God of Heaven and Earth.

Faith is the substance of things hoped for and the evidence of those things that are not seen with the natural eye. The presence and power of the Holy Spirit is the difference between living with no hope and living with the faith and hope to be transformed into the likeness of the One we worship. So, although we are aliens and strangers, we are to live in faith to inherit a home, a land, a country, and a Kingdom even as we are being transformed day by day from an image into a likeness.

As we are transformed, so too our thoughts and desires are transformed. Our minds are renewed by the continual washing of the water of the Word and fellowship with God. Paul told the believers in Ephesus that they too were once foreigners and aliens without hope, but now because of the blood of Jesus, they have been included in the Covenant with Israel. As a result, we don't live our lives without the hope of transformation, but as foreigners and aliens in this world who have been made sons and daughters, as the family of God looking to demonstrate and establish His Kingdom on Earth as it is in Heaven.

God's family is familiar with exile. Joseph, the son of Jacob, was rejected and even hated by his brothers because he was loved by his father. Joseph was different. He had dreams and visions. He had wisdom and a strange sense of the unseen world. I believe he was marked at an early age to be an imager of God who would demonstrate to the people of the wealthiest and most powerful nation on Earth that they worshiped false gods. I believe it was the compassion of YHVH for the nation of Egypt that eventually landed Joseph in a pit and resulted in his being sold to a caravan on its way to Egypt. He was born to be a deliverer, a savior, and an ambassador.

His life was fraught with trials and false accusations, but he was constantly sustained by hope and trust in the God of his fathers. He faithfully demonstrated the image and likeness of the Greater

Deliverer who would come after him to deliver the whole world. Although the image of Joseph was similar to all those around him, his likeness was of a different world. Joseph was exiled from his home, his family, and his people to deliver a nation from the bondage of slavery to false gods.

In the same way, Moses was exiled from his home, his family, and his people to be a faithful imager who would be made in the likeness of the God of Abraham, Isaac, and Jacob. His transformation took more time than Joseph's, but the early years of Moses's life were heavily influenced by the false worship of Egypt, surrounded by power and comfort. The trappings of this life can sometimes be a deeper pit to escape from than the lack of them. But by the time Moses was eighty years of age, he was ready to return to the house of Pharaoh and bear the image and likeness of the true God of Israel.

Daniel also was exiled from his home, his family, and his people—not because he was rebellious, but because the God of Israel would have compassion on Babylon and needed a faithful imager to demonstrate the likeness of the One True God. Nebuchadnezzar would prove to be a tough nut to crack, but like Pharaoh of Egypt, he would learn soon enough that he was nothing like the God of Daniel. This young man would be tested with food, comfort, false accusations, fire, and hungry lions, but the likeness could not be burned or beaten out of the imager. Daniel, like Joseph and Moses before him, had the power to save a nation.

Jesus was exiled from Heaven, not to save a nation but to deliver an entire planet. It has been proven time and again that although human beings are made in the image of God, we lack the power and even the will to be transformed into His likeness. We have short memories, and unless something affects us directly as individuals,

our attention spans are even shorter. We need help! The life and purpose of Jesus our Messiah was not only to *declare* who our God is, but
also to *demonstrate* who our God is. Then by His sacrifice, He acti-
vated the New Covenant, giving us the same hope and power to be
transformed into His likeness.

"Therefore, since we have such a hope, we are very bold" (2 Corinthians 3:12 NIV). Bold to what? Bold to believe, bold to hope, bold
to love, bold to declare and demonstrate, and bold to be imagers who
are not ashamed to be made in His likeness.

The encounter Pastor Stovall had on Passover has had a major
impact on the lives of everyone at Celebration Church, not the least
of which has been to make us bold. We are convicted and empowered
to worship boldly in spirit and in truth, to love others boldly with a
passion demonstrated by good deeds, to love the lost and the hurting,
to reach out to those around us, and to share the hope that we have.
We boldly stand against injustice and wickedness in our generation
and boldly support the nation of Israel, simply because our God
boldly loves her.

Music Unites Us

All throughout this book, I have told you that we have entered a
new time or era. The Prophet Amos declared that in the last days,
YHVH would raise up the fallen tent—tabernacle or *sukkah*—of
David and restore it as it used to be. This tabernacle or tent is being
reconstructed right now in our day as the sounds of a restored people
begin to wash over the sanctuaries and homes of God-lovers worldwide. These sounds are prophetic and anointed. Instead of speaking
to *us* in song, they speak to the throne and the King. They are bold to

declare what He says and are not afraid to use His name. Instead of the universal title of God or Lord, we are hearing the names Yahweh, El Shaddai, and more. One of the simple choruses that was taking the world by storm at the time of this writing came from Brazil. It simply repeats the name of Jesus in Hebrew, *Yeshua*, over and over again. It seems to me there is a place for the Jewish believer at a table where he or she is finally free once again to express truly biblical Jewish faith, and a big part of it is happening through music.

Music's impact is well documented in the Scriptures—from the mention of Jubal, the pioneer of all who played skillfully on the stringed instruments and the wind instruments noted in Genesis 4:21, to the opening of the heavens and the courts of Adonai in the Book of Revelation. One might argue that it was anointed, prophetic worship that brought down the mighty walls of Jericho, even though only one instrument was used. In 2 Chronicles 20, it was the singers sent out ahead of the armies of Jehoshaphat who won the day against a great multitude of Moabites and Ammonites:

> As they began singing and praising, Adonai set ambushes against the children of Ammon, Moab, and Mount Seir who had come against Judah, and they were defeated. (2 Chronicles 20:22 TLB)

At the end of that story, we discover that not only were the enemies of Israel defeated, but their enemies turned on each other and slaughtered themselves. This dramatic turning suggests to me that the force that had unified Israel's enemies was not natural or carnal, but rather an unseen adversary with great power to persuade and unite. It was likely a ruling, demonic force that could control the

actions of men. The lesson here is to see the role music played in
spiritual warfare in which we are engaged: "Our struggle is not against
flesh and blood, but against the rulers, against the powers, against the
worldly forces of this darkness, and against the spiritual forces of
wickedness in the heavenly places" (Ephesians 6:12 TLB).

Another place where Jewish worship music played a significant
role was in the first Temple in Jerusalem, built and dedicated by Solomon, the son of King David and Bathsheba:

> Then it came to pass that when the trumpeters and singers
> joined as one to extol and praise Adonai, and when the
> sound of the trumpets, cymbals and musical instruments
> and the praise of Adonai—"For He is good, for His mercy
> endures forever"—grew louder, the Temple, the House of
> Adonai, was filled with a cloud. The kohanim (priests)
> could not stand to minister because of the cloud, for the
> glory of Adonai filled the House of God. (2 Chronicles
> 5:13–14 TLB)

Another such scene of heavenly worship is recorded in the Book
of Revelation:

> And I saw something like a sea of glass mixed with fire,
> and those who had overcome the beast and his image and
> the number of his name standing by the sea of glass, hold-
> ing the harps of God. And they are singing the song of
> Moses, the servant of God and the song of the Lamb....
> And the Temple was filled with smoke from the glory of
> God and from His power. (Revelations 15:2–3 TLB)

It is impossible to read the Hebrew Scriptures and not see the foundational role music has played in the life of Israel and that it can potentially play in the lives of worshipers today. In the above passage, we see a wonderful theme of power and presence in praise. In Heaven there is perfect harmony and cohesion between the "song of Moses," the lawgiver, and the "song of the Lamb," the Covenant Maker. This passage begs the query: *Why do we here on Earth continue to build walls of doctrine that separate us from each other when Heaven sings a song of perfect unity?* After all, did not Messiah Yeshua break down the middle wall of partition?

I truly love the way sincere worship invokes the presence of Heaven. When that happens, revelation and understanding seem to flow like a river. In fact, this very unique attribute of Messianic worship continues to motivate and stimulate me after more than four decades of worship ministry. Since my humble beginnings with that Sears and Roebuck guitar, I have held on to my innate passion for music. The King has used it beyond my wildest expectations and continues to use this gift to further the Kingdom, just as He plans to utilize your unique talents for the glory of God and the Kingdom.

The thirst He gave me for music and His Kingdom leads me to consider worship in spirit and truth (John 4) using the Scriptures. Messianic worship music has always taken its cue directly from the Scriptures for lyrical content and inspiration. Several years ago, a wave of this kind of songwriting was hitting the Church. The simple choruses seemed to be an excellent way for people to memorize scripture verses in an effective way.

From the very beginning, this was the logical way for Messianic worship to develop because much of the material was extracted directly from the Psalms, the prophets, and the New Covenant, along with appropriate passages from the Siddur—(pronounced *sih-DOOR*), a collection of Jewish prayers used for worship, whose material is taken largely from the Hebrew Scriptures, the Book of Psalms, hymns, and blessings. The Siddur is a wonderful source of inspiration that I find very compelling, even though it is overlooked by much of the Church.

We discovered early on that worship derived from holy writ had a powerful effect on the atmosphere of the sanctuary, as well as on the heart of the worshiper. When we did this, we also discovered that the Spirit of prophecy and other giftings of the *Ruach* (Spirit) were powerfully present in corporate praise and worship. When we fill our hearts and mouths with the Word of the Living God and the praises of Adonai, He inhabits those praises so that even the very air we breathe is changed. Where He abides, all that He is becomes available by the *Ruach HaKodesh* (the Holy Spirit). Thus, we can minister with great confidence, almost prophesy at will, and worship all night if moved to do so.

Why is musical worship so fundamental? Why is it so powerful? King David explains it in one simple verse in Psalm 22:4: "Yet You are holy, enthroned on the praises of Israel" (TLB). Another translation says, "You inhabit the praises of your people Israel" (KJV), and yet another, "You *are* the praise of your people Israel" (NIV 1984, emphasis mine). The reason for these small differences is the use of the Hebrew word *yoshev*. It is a verb that means "to sit, dwell, inhabit," depending on where it is placed in the English sentence for translation. The same verse can be translated two different ways, giving a slightly different emphasis to the text. First, "You are enthroned as holy; (You are) the praise of Israel." Second, "You are holy; inhabiting or enthroned upon the praises of Israel."

Wherever you settle on the reading of this verse, it is impossible to separate His name, His power, and His presence from the praise of His people. So when we call upon the Name of Adonai in holiness, He inhabits the praises of His people. Where His presence abides, there is His glory, His power, His throne, His Kingdom—all that He is, is present. He inhabits our praises, our worship. All we really ever need is in Him.

When I speak about the power of praise and worship linked with the vehicle of music, I see a supernatural progression. Because God inhabits, or is enthroned upon, the praises of His people, what then is the effect of those praises and that presence on the worshiper? We read in Psalm 16:11: "Abundance of joys are in Your presence, eternal pleasures at Your right hand" (TLB). The Prophet Nehemiah tells us, "For the joy of Adonai is your strength" (Nehemiah 8:10b TLB).

Our praises provoke His presence, His pleasures, and joy, and that joy becomes our strength. If you want to be strong in the Lord and the power of His might, you need to be a worshiper whose mouth is full of praise. Psalm 118:15–16 declares: "Shouts of joy and victory are in the tents of the righteous: Adonai's right hand is mighty. Adonai's right hand is lifted high. Adonai's right hand is mighty" (TLB). I love these verses and sing them frequently.

I refer to these verses often when asked about all the noise and movement in Messianic praise. They have become a practical example of the outworking of corporate praise and worship. You may be asking, *Paul, what do you mean by that?* I am fond of asking a question to answer a question, so I ask you: Where is there no singing, no shouting, no rejoicing? The answer: In the tents of the defeated. You'll find no celebration in a graveyard, where there is no victory and seemingly no presence of Adonai.

Messianic worship has always been a platform for dance, banners, the waving of flags, sounding shofars and tambourines, shouts of joy, and more. Where there is true worship, there is His presence. Where His presence dwells, there is the fullness of joy. As Nehemiah tells us, joy begets strength, and round and round the circle goes, from praise to presence, to joy to strength, and so forth until the *amen* is sounded.

Messianic Worship Reborn

Modern Messianic praise and worship is celebrating a rebirth after some fifty years or so, by my estimation. Messianic worship music is a unique expression that I have come to love not only for its Scripture content, but also for its focus and intent. Where much of today's contemporary Christian music focuses on the worshiper and his or her needs, Messianic worship focuses on the One we worship, who is our source and strength. For me, it is a matter of pronouns. Instead of "I need" or "We are," the pronouns change to "You alone are holy" and "Yeshua, You are Lord." I characterize Messianic praise and worship as being directed toward the throne and the One who sits there.

Direct quotes from the Scriptures make great opening lines for our material. "Lord God of Abraham, Isaac, and Israel, let it be known today that You are God...." (1 Kings 18:36 NKJV) is a quote from Elijah's famous showdown with the priests of Baal on Mount Carmel, as well as the opening line of the song that leads my recording of *The Watchman* (2005). The very next song on the CD proclaims, "Adonai, You alone are God, every tongue will cry, Adonai." You get the picture. We enter His gates with "Thank you" (*todah*) in our mouths and His courts with holy hands lifted up in praise (*t'hilah*).

Messianic worship music is also direct, even masculine to my way of thinking. It is strong, Bible-based, yet also tender and sensitive, like a father with his child. It is poignant and instructive, never compromising for a cultural expression, unashamed of its roots, and unafraid of what others might think. The intention is always to bow down before a King and provoke His presence with passion and love.

Messianic music is the heart of King David expressed through a New Covenant lens of hearing, seeing, and understanding. Propagating and ministering this worship, message, and ministry have been my life's passion and focus for the past forty years. It will continue to challenge and engage me for the rest of my life.

Some churchmen have misunderstood the reason for my passion and purpose, saying I desire to re-erect the middle wall of partition that the Messiah destroyed by the cross. Nothing could be further from the truth. The goal is the unity and peace that come only by the presence of the Prince of Peace; we want only to see all Israel saved and the Church restored. May the God of Abraham, Isaac, and Israel give us enough grace and love to finish our race with strength and to hear those blessed words, "Well done, good and faithful servant."

PROPHECY FULFILLED

I have seen firsthand the power of the unity of God's covenantal blessing. All the Children of Abraham are coming together in our own day like never before. In Genesis 12:3, we find the well-known words of God to Abram: "I will bless those who bless you...and every family on earth will be blessed through you" (NIV). In Chapter 16, we learn that Abraham's first son, Ishmael, has been born. In Chapter 17, both Ishmael and Abraham are circumcised as belonging to the

Lord. Four chapters later, Isaac is born while Ishmael and his Egyptian mother, Hagar, are forced out of the family tent by Sarah's jealousy. Although every family on Earth would be blessed by Abraham's faith, his own family would suffer violence and division for many generations to come.

During the 2020 Passover gathering on Zoom, a startling and amazing revelation of God's faithfulness overtook us all as we realized that the descendants of Isaac and Ishmael were returning to the family table and the New Covenant of the Lamb. It was a partial fulfillment of the promise to Abraham and Isaac from way back in Genesis 22.

Tears of love and compassion flowed like a river that evening when we remembered that Ishmael was Abraham's firstborn son. He was the first of Abraham's sons to be circumcised and by right of law had the birthright of the double-portion inheritance. Ishmael was also one of only three people in all the Scriptures to be named before he was born. The others were Yohanan (John the Baptist) and Yeshua Himself. And finally, the blessing of Abraham that would touch "every family on Earth" would find its way to his own house as well. Ishmael and Isaac would return to the table at an appointed time to break bread and remember the promise, to pray and bless each other in covenant love.

Another startling revelation emerging from our Passover meeting was the rebuilding of the Isaiah 19 Highway. The Lord spoke through the Prophet Isaiah, saying:

> In that day there will be a highway from Egypt to Assyria.... The Egyptians and Assyrians will worship together. In that day Israel will be a third with Egypt and Assyria, a blessing on the earth. The Lord Almighty will bless them, saying,

"Blessed be Egypt my people, Assyria my handiwork, and Israel my inheritance." (Isaiah 19:23–25 NIV)

On a Zoom call later that year, as the world was filled with confusion, shutdowns, isolation, and fear, a quick glance around the screen filled with Arab, Jew, and Gentile faces told us that we were all a part of something very special—of a prophecy fulfilled. We worshiped with family we had never met from all across the ancient world. They were all there: Iraq, Iran, Turkey, Syria, Lebanon, Egypt, and Israel. We heard from Arab brothers and sisters who had been praying for that day for decades. I spoke with young Arab brothers and sisters who told me they have loved my music their whole lives and used it to learn a little Hebrew from the "Holy Land." The warmth of meeting lost family members completely overshadowed any sense of animosity or insecurity.

Months later we would feel the power of covenant and peace as Arab nations began to announce that they would normalize relationships with Israel. We were actually on one of our weekly Zoom calls when the announcement came that the United Arab Emirates would be the first to welcome Israeli Prime Minister Benjamin Netanyahu to begin talks of peace. Bahrain soon followed suit, then Sudan, and many others would follow. The ancient and seemingly impossible prophecies of Isaiah were coming to pass right before our eyes...on *moedim*, the appointed times of the Lord.

LET THE LION ROAR

Throughout all of human history, all of us—Jew and Gentile alike—have run from our Father. As Jesus demonstrated in the

Parable of the Prodigal Son (Matthew 15:11–32), we have all rebelled against our Father and wallowed with the swine. When we returned home, our Father forgave us, but our brothers chafed over the exceptional grace we were shown.

That was then. This is now.

Now YWVH's children are forgiving one another, embracing lost brothers and sisters, and rejoicing in being redeemed by the same Jewish Messiah. Who knows what threats we may face in the near future? Perhaps antisemitism will rage once again, or the Bible will be torched in the streets as it was in the 1930s. Who can say? Whatever may come, we will endure, united under one hope: "Yeshua, a light of revelation to the Gentiles, and the glory of Your people Israel."

The house, once divided, is being rebuilt. The family is returning to the healing of Shabbat, the sanctity of the Table, the joys of His presence in worship, and the hope of the Messiah as the Kingdom comes and the Lion of Judah roars from His holy hill.

Empires come and go. Nations rise and fall. But our Heavenly Father will never scatter us again. The King is coming back. Let His people rejoice. Come to the table of covenant, to the Bread of Life and the Cup of Redemption. Here the Prince of Peace and the Lord of the Sabbath has prepared a place for all. The times are changing. The Lion of Judah is on the move. The Spirit and the Bride say, "Come." And the earth replies, "Even so, come Lord Jesus."

AFTERWORD

I n John 4, Jesus has His famous conversation with the Samaritan woman at a well. It is so interesting to me that this woman who does not seem to have a relationship with God is eager to ask a question about worship. She wants to know where she should worship. Yeshua walks her back to the real question: *Whom* should we worship?

We have created many resources to help you worship the Father in spirit and in truth. At our website (WilburMinistries.com), you will find books, recordings, teachings, and more. We also have a new free Wilbur Ministries app available in your favorite app store. It has a lot of media that will instruct and demonstrate many of the special celebrations I have written about here.

Please take advantage of all these resources which we have created to turn your home into a sanctuary. Any space can become a sanctuary when we as priests of the New Covenant invite the presence of the Living God. Taste and see.

Feasts of the Kingdom

W e have been given more than just the Sabbath to remind us of our calling and purpose. God also gave Israel many feasts and holidays to remember and keep holy. These feasts occur all throughout the year and are intended for the whole family of God, both Jews and Gentiles. I invite you to taste and see these feasts of the Kingdom for yourself:

- **Passover Feast:** The Passover is Israel's celebration of deliverance from slavery in Egypt through great miracles, signs, and wonders. Jesus celebrated this meal with His disciples, which has come to be known as "The Last Supper" or communion. I have also come to see this feast in a larger expression, as the Lord made a marriage proposal to all who would leave Egypt and share in a wedding in the desert at Mount Sinai.
- **Feast of Unleavened Bread:** The seven days following Passover are called the Feast of Unleavened Bread, which is a fast and a feast. For seven days, there is to be no food consumed with leaven (yeast), and every meal has matzo at its center. Because of the short time the Israelites had to prepare to leave Egypt, God told them to make bread in haste without yeast and use it to remember His

deliverance from slavery. This bread is also bruised, striped, and pierced. It is the very same bread Jesus used at the Last Supper when He said, "This is my body which is given for you."

- **Feast of First Fruits:** During the Feast of Unleavened Bread comes the Feast of First Fruits. The Lord instructed that First Fruits be one of three major harvest times. In 1 Corinthians 15:20, the Apostle Paul states, "But Christ has indeed been raised from the dead, the first fruits of those who have fallen asleep" (NIV). Jesus was raised from the tomb on the Feast of First Fruits, and resurrection life is guaranteed for all those who trust in Him. What an incredible picture of the Lord's grace and love displayed for all to see.

- **Feast of Pentecost** or **Shavuot:** The Hebrew word *Shavuot* is the word for "weeks" in the English language and celebrates the day the Torah was given to Moses and the citizens of the Kingdom. We get the name "Pentecost" from the Greek *Pentékonta*, which means "fifty," as the feast happens fifty days after Passover. It is so special that it was on this feast that the promised Holy Spirit was poured out on the 120 worshipers in the Upper Room. Appointed times have special surprises for those who are watchful.

- **Feast of Trumpets:** The Feast of Trumpets is the first of the fall holidays and is celebrated at the beginning of Tishri, the seventh month of the biblical calendar and the first month of the civil calendar. As the first month of the civil year, this feast also serves as the

Jewish New Year. The Feast of Trumpets marks the beginning of the ten holiest days of the Jewish year. These "Ten Days of Awe" are a time for personal reflec tion on our relationship with God. Could this day for sounding trumpets be prophetically linked to the return of the Lord as Paul describes it in 1 Thessalonians 4:16–17?

- **Yom Kippur:** Next on the fall feast calendar (September through October) is Yom Kippur, or the Day of Atonement, where there is fasting, prayer, and a whole day for confession of sin. This is about preparing our hearts for the second coming of the Messiah. In biblical times, this was the only day each year that the high priest could enter the Holy of Holies, the innermost room of the Temple. On this day, the priest would enter the Lord's presence, and through a series of specific steps and blood sacrifices, he would make atonement for himself and all the people. The Day of Atonement marks the completion of the "Ten Days of Awe," which begins with the Feast of Trumpets. These ten days are dedicated to repentance, prayer, and charity, and serve to set the stage for this most solemn day of the year. More than any other day, the Day of Atonement is a time to seek the Lord. Many believe that this is the day Jesus will return and take up His throne in Jerusalem.

- **Feast of Tabernacles:** The Feast of Tabernacles, or Feast of Booths, is the third and final fall feast. In stark contrast to the solemnity of the Day of Atonement, it's a time for joyous celebrations among God's people. It is held to remember the forty years the Israelites spent wandering in the desert, during which time the Lord provided for them in every way. This is also one of the three times God commands His people not to appear before Him empty-handed. Instead of getting caught up in the desire for more, God is reminding us that this earth is not our home, and we should not be distracted by the things of this world. Like the Israelites, we are also on a journey to our own eternal Promised Land, and we should look to God alone as our shelter and comfort. This is the final harvest of the year, and many believe it is the feast that inspired our own national celebration of Thanksgiving.

If this small taste of the Kingdom's feasts and divine traditions has inspired you to continue to dig deeper and witness the revelation of these holy times, then I strongly encourage you to visit our website (WilburMinistries.com). There you will find more resources regarding the feasts, Sabbath, and "appointed times" our Father has given us to share and observe as a Covenant family. "Taste and see that the Lord is good" (Psalms 34:8 NIV).